The Radical Advocacy

of Wendell Phillips

AMERICAN ABOLITIONISM AND ANTISLAVERY
John David Smith, series editor

The Radical Advocacy of

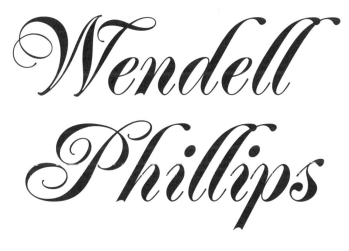

Wendell Phillips

Abolitionism, Democracy, and Public Interest Law

PETER CHARLES HOFFER

THE KENT STATE UNIVERSITY PRESS

Kent, Ohio

Contents

Public Interest Lawyering and Strong Democratic Positivism

*B*oston's Wendell Phillips (1811–1884) is best known as a fierce and dedicated abolitionist orator. His funeral in Boston brought together the rich and poor, white and Black, the highbrow and the low born to celebrate his role in the demise of slavery. Eulogists in the former Confederate states joined in the chorus, admitting that they had hated him at one time. That admission highlights a remarkable fact—in his day no public figure was so contradictory and so elusive than Phillips. In person he could be self-deprecating and gentle, but few public men were more acerbic. His speeches and writings rivaled the philippics of Cicero. Those who attended his many public talks—over a thousand in his lifetime— were almost invariably impressed with his delivery and his demeanor. Clever, keen, even brilliant, concluded Bronson Alcott. Chauncey Depew, who had also heard Henry Clay and Daniel Webster speak, declared that Phillips was their superior. When the aged Henry Wadsworth Longfellow left the platform he had shared with Phillips in 1881, the poet laureate was heard to say, "Marvelous and delightful, but preposterous from beginning to end." Nor was the contradiction a pose—Phillips really was an enigma, then and now. Throughout his career, he was an agitator extraordinaire. Shortly before the Civil War erupted, when he demanded that Massachusetts leave the Union and insisted that the Constitution must be cast aside, he had to hire bodyguards to walk from a lecture hall.

Seeming evidence of his contrarian nature, instead these contradictions reflected the qualities of his public interest lawyering and his adoption of the jurisprudence of strong democracy.[1]

Phillips was a lawyer, but a lawyer of a different stripe from his contemporaries. For Phillips, the law was more than practice in an office or a courtroom. It was more than mastery of a body of information. It was a way of thinking, of arguing, of explaining. His father and two of his older brothers were practicing lawyers. Phillips attended Harvard Law School for three years. He finished the course and graduated. His mentor there was Joseph Story, whose lectures were published as commentaries on American law. Once again, there were contradictions. Phillips's practice—first in Lowell, Massachusetts and then in Boston—did not flourish. He did not put into practice the energy it required. It bored him. If he found it unappealing, he nevertheless spent much time with Harvard classmates such as Charles Sumner, whose law practice also languished. But the two men must have discussed how law could change the world, for in subsequent years that is exactly what they essayed.[2]

More contradictions in Phillips's legal career followed. James Redpath, himself a strong abolitionist who knew Phillips, said that Phillips originally hesitated to sign the oath to the Constitution required of members of the bar, then did so. In 1842, he publicly refused to swear the oath. But he never renounced his allegiance to the Massachusetts state constitution or membership in its bar. Until 1861, he called for Massachusetts to leave the Union, for so long as it remained in the Union, it was tainted by the sin of slavery. Then he changed his mind, and supported the Union and the federal Constitution in the Civil War. Not drawn to running for office or serving in it (with one notable exception), Phillips never hesitated to express his political opinions. But he was never a politician.[3]

In one very important way, however, Phillips was consistent. For Phillips, abolitionism—the total eradication of slavery, as opposed to antislavery, the belief that slavery was wrong—was always a legal campaign, driven by what he called an "agitational rationale," and he was at the center of that campaign. He believed, consistently and profoundly, in what later jurists would call the "rule of law." But this was not the rule of courts and legislatures, or the "quibbles" of courtroom litigators. It was a law that rested on the will of the whole people, properly instructed. This is what I have called the philosophy of strong democracy—a faith that the participation of the many will fashion laws that are just for all.[4]

It was this vision of law that brought coherence and power to what seemed his many contradictions. To aid his activism, Phillips fashioned himself into America's first public interest lawyer. In doing so, Phillips adopted the legal positivist jurisprudence of the English jurist John Austin (about which more momentarily). Phillips's jurisprudence rested in turn on his faith in American democracy, but only a "strong democracy"—a polity in which all the people, regardless of race, gender, or class, take part.

Most modern commentators date the rise of public interest advocacy to the Progressive Era, in particular to the appearance of "cause" organizations such as the National Association for the Advancement of Colored People (NAACP) and the American Civil Liberties Union (ACLU), or with the activities of the National Lawyers Guild. The term public interest advocacy came into prominence in the 1960s with the appearance of public interest law firms. Groups such as the Southern Poverty Law Center engaged in both public interest and cause lawyering. Individual "cause lawyers" also advocated for defendants in a variety of public capacities. Some, such as William Kunstler, associated themselves with the radical-left defendants they represented. As critical of the legal and political establishment as they were, they served their clients in court in traditional fashion. Phillips's unpaid advocacy of the civil rights of people of color, women, and working people anticipated the central concerns of the Progressive Era reform associations and modern public interest law firms; thus, he deserves credit for pioneering the roles of modern activist lawyering.[5]

Lawyers working to end homelessness identify themselves as the descendants of the abolitionists. So do lawyers working to undo the carceral state. Today, anyone familiar with Ralph Nader will recognize the passion and commitment that public interest lawyers bring to their profession. Like Phillips, Nader and his allies had a strong antipathy to the state, "a profound and pervasive distrust of government," suspecting it of working hand and hand with unsavory private interests. On October 10, 2019, Nader told a gathering at Harvard Law School, "Lawlessness is the norm when it comes to the rich and powerful, which is why when you come to this law school you should have a choice. Do you want to be a traditional lawyer who drafts contracts, deeds, and represents corporations, or do you want to focus on lawlessness, which is the norm?" Change the subject from the lawlessness of the rich and powerful to the lawlessness of the enslaver and the speaker might have been Phillips. (Actually, in his last public address, to the Harvard chapter of Phi Beta Kappa, on February 2, 1881, Phillips did say almost the exact same thing as Nader.) Nader pursued public office. With one exception, Phillips did not. Nader's crusade against corporate greed won converts and changed laws. Phillips's crusades against slavery and the oppression of women, and for immigrants' and workers' rights did not always bring immediate results. But his commitment was as strong and consistent as Nader's.[6]

The achievements of the modern "cause" and public interest lawyers would have been possible without the precedent of Phillips's lawyering, but that should not deprive him of the credit of being the first of the kind. Practicing without remuneration from clients, he did what public interest lawyers do: create public consciousness of basic ills; stir consciences; and direct public officials toward needed reform. His demand for dynamic change— without his ferocious ad hominem attacks on opponents—is their credo. Phillips's early career trajectory fits the model of the 1960s young lawyer eager to find justice for the disadvantaged. So too, his incipient jurisprudence of strong democratic positivism reset the agenda for legal thinking in later generations—although Phillips' pioneering role in that conceptualization is often overlooked.[7]

. . .

Phillips was a positivist, unlike many in his profession at that time. The antebellum period was marked by a strong belief in the natural-law foundations of jurisprudence. During the Revolutionary Era, this natural law expressed itself in effusive and global pronouncements on liberty. In the early nineteenth century, it became something that inhered in the individual bosom, and because of the rise of individualism, natural rights jurisprudence gained a second wind. Property rights stood at the center of this revival, as jurists saw in private property a reflection of deeper natural law currents.[8]

By contrast, in its inception in the work of the English jurist John Austin, legal positivism of a most brutal kind was indifferent to individualism. Austin was aware that few read his lectures, published in 1832, and that those who had were not impressed. But his message in them was clear: "Every positive law, or rule of positive law, exists as such by the pleasure of the sovereign." The law was the "command" of the state and must be obeyed. It was not necessarily democratic. It was not a source or an expression of morals.[9]

Phillips did not subscribe to that particular version of positivism. He believed in a strongly democratic positivism, that is, he believed that good law aligned with the will of the people. "This land is the normal school— the nation set by God to try the experiment of popular education, popular government, to smooth the obstacles, discover the dangers, guard against the perils, facilitate the progress, help forward the hopes and the steps of the race." This philosophy of law created a quandary for the abolitionists, for it seemed that the majority in the North, and even more in the white South, believed that slave law was the will of the people. Phillips did not accept that view. Over and over he argued that the people must be educated to see the wrong in slavery. They must change the laws. This failing, the people must abandon the state, in this case the federal government and its fundamental law—the Constitution.[10]

For Phillips, public interest lawyering and strong democratic positivism were intimately related. In his thinking and his activities, they evolved together. They were logically interlocking, for the public interest lawyer pleaded his cause to the democracy, on the assumption that the basis of obedience to law lay in public opinion. What was more, in both public interest lawyering and fashioning a strong democratic positivism, his commitment to democracy and his jurisprudence of positivism were interrelated. But in another of Phillips's storied contradictions, he warned that living "under" public opinion in slavery times was never an easy matter.[11]

In his final public address, Phillips told the Phi Beta Kappa chapter of Harvard College, "The agitator must stand outside of organizations, with no bread to earn, no candidate to elect, no party to save, no object but truth—to tear a question open and riddle it with truth. In all modern constitutional governments, agitation is the only peaceful method of progress." He walked his talk, having spent the previous twenty years urging Congress and the president to legislate social and economic equality for the freed slaves.[12]

. . .

The major sources for this study are Phillips's orations, speeches, and other public utterances. In 1863, he yielded to the importuning of his admirers and revised his speeches for publication. He was contemplating a second set at the time of his death; it was published in 1891 and overlapped the first series in time. What struck me as I first encountered these speeches is that unlike almost all other abolitionists, Phillips did not spend the bulk of his time on the evils of slavery. He did not dwell on the abuses of the enslavers. He did not present real-life stories of enslaved people. He assumed they were true but offered no firsthand evidence. His target was the Northerner who condoned slavery or abetted it. This was the person (or institution) that the law could reach. Those whom the law could not reach—Southern states and Southern enslavers—he excoriated, but only in passing.[13]

I frame my analysis of individual speeches in four contexts: Phillips's previous utterances; Phillips's life at the time he made each speech; the state of the nation at the time he made the speech; and the place of the speech in this book. Like a picture frame, the four approaches touch one another but are distinct. The first and third framing devices grow from Phillips's own rhetorical style. He commented on the issues, events, and people of the day as they arose, especially during his stint as an editorial writer for the *National Anti-Slavery Standard* after the Civil War. Thus his addresses and his editorials form a narrative of the country's struggle with racism and other public evils. The second frame holds the first and third in place. He included his own experiences in each speech and referred back to earlier addresses. With the rest of the Boston abolitionist party, he watched John Quincy Adams's attempt to lift the gag rule on antislavery petitions in the House of Representatives. Motivated by—indeed, perhaps imagining himself as—Adams, he leaped into the public debate on the gag rule, and then on the assassination of the abolitionist Elijah Lovejoy. He welcomed the British antislavery advocate George Thompson. Not every public address, but all the important ones, always followed a momentous event in the history of antislavery. Read together, in sequence, they become evidence of Phillips's development of public interest lawyering and its central doctrine of strong democratic positivism. The last of the framing devices is my choice of particular speeches to explore. Phillips gave dozens of speeches. By selecting and, within selections, by analyzing his ideas I have tried to set the development of his advocacy in its clearest framework.[14]

Some characteristics of my presentation of Phillips's speeches pose obstacles to their analysis. Like the lectures a college instructor delivers over a long career, the speehes repeat material—inescapable, considering the number of speeches Phillips gave. The quality of his performance made them seem fresh to his audiences, but reading them one after the other, one notices the repetition. A second characteristic makes tracing the threads of his argument difficult. Because Phillips did not speak from notes, his speeches wandered. For his audiences, the asides, anecdotes, references and other deviations from the subject at hand were part of the performance. Reading the same content, one has trouble following his train of thought: hearing and reading are different sensory experiences. Third, listening to him from the floor of the lecture hall or from its stage, men like Ralph Waldo Emerson were amazed at the fluidity and grace of his delivery in the face of hostile audiences. Calm, conversational, his posture aristocratic, Phillips had a command of New England anecdotes that poured oil on the tempests of the most troubled gatherings. At the same time, he indulged in expressions of disdain, snide remarks, and cutting language. He regularly attacked the character and the conduct of those with whom he disagreed. Although this excess may have been a byproduct of his extemporaneous style of speaking, the impact of his choice of words stung the objects of his vitriol. That makes reading them unpleasant.[15]

Nevertheless, with the entire corpus of Phillips's public addresses at hand, a scholarly observer will see in them an evolution of his thinking that contemporaries would have missed. Where they saw contradictions and occasional unpleasantries, greater distance and access to the totality of his speeches reveals originality and coherence. At least that is what I found. But there is always the danger that the historians' access to sources may harbor a disadvantage. Other accounts of Phillips's thinking find him typical of the romantic moralism of his age, a latter-day puritan perfectionist, and an anti-institutional idealist. Some biographers note that this conservative Boston Brahmin was radicalized by his contact with the "Boston Clique" of his spouse, Ann Green, and then by William Lloyd Garrison. Still others find a "professional reformer" who vanished behind a wall of words. Surely Phillips was all of these, to some extent, at various times, to which I add here a public interest lawyer and an advocate of strong democratic positivism.[16]

CHAPTER 1

Abolitionist

Wendell Phillips was born on November 29, 1811, on the eve of the War of 1812. The war was brought on by the failure of Jeffersonian Republican diplomacy and the obstinate refusal of Europe's warring powers to accede to American neutrality. The war would try the spirit and diminish the income of Boston's mercantile and professional elite, to which his family belonged. It hit the commercial activities of the Bostonians hardest. They would join in a regional protest that culminated in the Hartford Convention of 1814—a meeting over whose delegates the prospect of secession hovered as a legitimate if ultimate form of protest.[1]

Phillips's family pedigree was to him both a blessing and a curse. The Phillipses had a long and storied history in the commonwealth; his father, the lawyer John Phillips, was wealthy, respected, and politically connected. Belonging to what was later called the Brahmin aristocracy, the family epitomized the combination of private enterprise and public reputation in New England. Wendell was the eighth child of nine, however, and that meant that family time and money had to be spread around parsimoniously. Still, there were servants, cousins, aunts, and friends of the family—a reminder that the Beacon Hill community was well endowed. And no one—especially his mother, Sarah—hesitated to remind him of his status and the obligations it entailed. One must be a gentleman; one must adhere to a code of public service; and one must learn manhood's ways.[2]

Wendell was twelve when his father suddenly died. There were other male role models, however. He had four older brothers, Thomas, John, Samuel, and George, two of whom, Thomas and George, would go on to become lawyers and one, John Charles, a clergyman. They set an example that would be difficult to surpass. George was born one year before Wendell, and so the attention that might have gone to the youngest son had to be shared. Samuel Phillips, born ten years before Wendell, died in 1817, a reminder that life was precarious, even for the wellborn. With adult male responsibilities closing in as his adolescence began, how were he, and his class, to deal with the rapidly changing world of Beacon Hill? How were the genteel to respond to the raucous enjoyments and employments of the hoi polloi at their doorsteps in the city? After all, Boston was a seafaring town, and no one was rougher in their manners than sailors ashore and dockworkers in the taverns that surrounded the family mansion. What followed, then, was an uncertain manhood, given on the one hand to the pleasures and honors of Brahmin society, and on the other to the self-discipline required to maintain the advantages of class and status. At Boston Latin School, where he started when he was eleven, he showed both his intellectual curiosity and his penchant for gentlemanly posturing in front of an audience. As a speaker, he was a natural. And he loved it.[3]

In a composition book he kept as a teenager at the Latin School (Puritans and scions of Puritans always kept diaries to remind themselves that salvation was not to be had for good works alone), he warned himself and his young companions of the seductive dangers of having and exercising power. In later years he would decline public office (only once reversing himself and declaring as an independent temperance and labor reform candidate for governor of Massachusetts), but when he read the composition book essay to his Latin School classmates, he was clearly referring to himself. Thomas Appleton, a school chum and playmate, remembered how Phillips delighted in reciting scraps of famous speeches from memory to his friends, with a stage presence that belied his years. From his youth, Appleton recalled, Phillips was always an "eloqutionist [*sic*]."[4]

Public speaking was a popular feature of antebellum Boston culture and something of a celebrity turn, with famous orators bringing out crowds of both the highbrow and the lowborn. Attending these lectures was Wendell's favorite pastime. Most weeks one could find a lecture at Faneuil Hall, the City Hall, various churches, the Masonic Temple, Chauncy Hall, and later the Odeon. The latter, a concert hall and lecture hall, opened in 1832, and featured over twelve hundred seats—all upholstered—in a semicircle facing the raised stage. A gallery completed the interior. In 1829, the city luminaries founded the Boston Lyceum, an association that sponsored free public lectures all over the city. Of course the great Daniel Webster was routinely called on to give public anniversary addresses, making himself visible everywhere in the public eye. His oratorical style was classical; like Cicero, he mixed praise and scorn, using his voice and gestures like musical instruments. Not a Boston Brahmin but a tavern keeper's son from rural New Hampshire, he had moved his law practice to Boston in 1805 and was thereafter associated with its interests. Close behind in popular acclaim were Edward Everett and William Ellery Channing. Everett was very much a Brahmin. Channing came from solid but lower-status stock in Rhode Island. Both were Unitarian ministers, and outside of the meeting house, they lectured on political topics, the arts, and, as it happened, antislavery. Both united eloquence and learning. Phillips had many fine examples to follow were he to become a public speaker.[5]

His deceased father's influence still fell like a long shadow over Wendell. But his father's Puritan religion was giving way in the son to a more emotional style of worship—the Second Great Awakening—and at the Latin School, Phillips showed some inclination to join in its enthusiasm. He did not pursue the ministry, however, as his brother John Charles did. He was also influenced by the rise of a national literature. It was the early days of Boston's claim to be the Athens of America. The young Wendell swayed back and forth according to the cultural impulses of the Jacksonian era. Finally, he began to interest himself in his family's and his city's history as a way of reassuring himself of his own role in that history.[6]

Phillips matriculated at Harvard College in 1827. All his boyhood friends went there, and he had no trouble passing the entrance examinations. Handsome, athletic, and sociable, he was only a fair student, but his classmates admired him. A study of his commonplace book and his orations, as well as the recollections of his classmates, shows a restrained young man, determined to do good and self-aware to the extent that he knew he was an able public speaker. He developed a theory of eloquence, mixing personal belief, passion, and elite self-satisfaction. He remained family proud, and in his later career he would cite the achievements of great New Englanders. Into this mix he poured his somewhat eclectic study of history, praising England and derogating France. His heroes were all English, allied by culture and blood to his own family. In this sense, his reading of history was a reading of his own pedigree.[7]

Whether his admonitions to himself on the nature of public speaking and the uses of history amounted to a personal philosophy of republican individualism, or simply an extended adolescent love of fantasy, is unclear. One may suspect that the mature Phillips was never a complete man. It was as though at some point his emotional development stopped short. Onstage, speaking before an audience, he was fully alive. He drew energy and assurance from his public. Offstage, away from the crowd, he was still the fatherless child, given to dramatic excess. His moralism was brittle, his empathetic qualities shallow. He declared that he loved the underdog, the enslaved, the wretch, and the poor, but he never walked among them or visited where they lived. When the occasion arose, he did encourage the publication of firsthand accounts. His support was sincere but condescending. For the publication of Frederick Douglass's *Narrative* (1845) Phillips wrote, "We have been left long enough to gather the character of slavery, from the involuntary evidence of the masters. . . . [Now w]e have known you long and can put the most entire confidence in your truth, candor and sincerity. . . . [But a]fter all, I shall read your book with trembling for you," for Douglass was still a runaway, and no runaway was ever truly safe.[8]

Phillips entered Harvard Law School in 1831. As he admitted, somewhat wryly, in 1850, he was among those who were "bred to the bar," though he did not earn his bread there. His father and brothers were lawyers, but Harvard Law School—in fact, all law schools in America—was something new. At first, the law school, itself only twenty-four years old, was little more than a lectureship endowed by the Massachusetts appeals court justice Isaac Parker and the university professor of law Asahel Stearns. The lecture method remained the rule when Parker and Stearns ended their tenures (in 1827 and 1829, respectively). In 1827, Justice Joseph Story was appointed the Nathan Dane Professor and John Hooker Ashmun the Royall Professor. Simon Greenleaf replaced the deceased Ashmun in 1833. A new building, Dane Hall, was allotted to the school in 1831, and the relative handful of students (one in 1827, twenty-seven in 1829, and forty-two in 1832) grew to over 160 by the end of Story's tenure in 1845. Story was a "collector of young men," including Charles Sumner, Richard Henry Dana, and Phillips. Story was an early and avid promoter of the school and is generally credited with its remarkable growth. He and Greenleaf advertised in newspapers and magazines all over the country, attempting to recruit a nationwide class. They prepared a prospectus for incoming students that stressed the library and the textbook-lecture method. Once students entered in the classroom, however, the method of teaching was lecture and recitation, with a great deal of outside reading in legal treatises and case reports. The overall goal was the promotion of the "scientific study of law."[9]

Story may or may not have read John Austin's *Province of Jurisprudence*. Austin's book was published in 1832, but no references to it appear in any of Story's commentaries on the law, written from 1832 to 1836. Austin's project of making the study of law scientific was the rage of the era, however, and part of that project was fidelity to positive law. This certainly was Story's credo as well, but Story also believed in natural law's part in adjudication. Thus when the two came into conflict in slavery cases, in both *United States v.* Amistad (1841) and *Prigg v. Pennsylvania* (1842), cases whose results seemed to be at odds, Story rested his opinion on strict fidelity to legal texts. Whether Story was comfortable with the contradictions, or, as his son and biographer wrote, agonized over them, Phillips was not mollified. His eulogy of Story condemned his former teacher for his opinion in *Prigg v. Pennsylvania* (1842), which voided the state's antikidnapping law.[10]

After obtaining his Bachelor of Laws degree in 1834, Phillips continued to study informally with his former classmate Thomas Hopkinson. They shared a practice in Lowell, Massachusetts, twenty miles outside of Boston. The arrangement did not last, and in 1835 Phillips returned to Boston. He had *passed the bar*, a phrase going back to old English lawyering, when those who could argue before the king's court stood inside the "bar" separating the students from the practitioners (called barristers). Introduced into American law in the eighteenth century, the bar association, a professional organization chartered by each state, required prospective members to swear an oath to preserve the state constitution and the federal Constitution. (This followed the requirement in Article VI, section 3 of the federal Constitution, that all federal and state officials had to take an oath to preserve and defend it. Nothing in that oath said anything about the Union.) Lawyers are officers of the court and bound by such oaths. Every bar has a code of ethics to which its members must adhere. Apparently, Phillips observed all of these practices.[11]

The historian Dean Grodzins has found that Phillips belonged to the Middlesex and Suffolk County bar associations and did not drop those affiliations in later years. He was listed in the *Boston Directory*, a business reference work, as a "counsellor," having an office in Boston in 1850, 1851, 1855, 1856, and 1861 at 26 Essex Street (in fact his home). A law review piece from 1872 asserted that Phillips remained a member of the county bar. He may or may not have practiced law in some form there. Or the entry may simply be due to negligence of the directory compiler, George Adams. Phillips had publicly renounced his profession ten years earlier. Still, he did not call the error—if error it was—to the compiler's attention.[12]

What happened, or did not happen, in Lowell to drive Phillips back to Boston remains a mystery. Lowell was a company town on the banks of the Merrimac River by Pawtucket Falls. The setting was a perfect spot for textile mills. Young women from nearby farms found a place in the many factories that turned raw cotton into fabric and clothing. Lowell was typical of antebellum commercial New England—combining cheap labor, southern cotton, and British technology put to use by American capitalists. For all of those reasons, it could not have been appealing to Phillips, whose Boston pedigree was everything that bustling Lowell was not. Would he serve the new masters of the nation's economy? The essence of the factory world was the exploitation of workers, particularly the farm girls housed in dormitories and summoned to the dangerous machinery by the factory bells. Nor did he show at this time the attachment to the laboring classes that he would demonstrate a decade later. For whatever reason, Phillips found practice in Lowell abhorrent. The irony was that the city and the mills were the work of Francis Cabot Lowell, whose genealogy was as storied and whose family was as elite as Phillips's own.[13]

The disappointing pattern of the Lowell practice was repeated in Boston. Phillips's practice there did not flourish, either. He told his friend Thomas Appleton that he had no clients. Phillips did not even have his own office in the city. He rented desk room at a workspace in a building on Court Street. The location was apt—next to the state courthouse and the city prison. (The street was previously called Prison Lane.) Whether or not anyone came to him seeking legal aid, he was indifferent to his professional advancement. He did not need the fees, at any rate. If practice did not appeal to him, and he did not thrive it in, the law stuck to him, as history and rhetoric had in his youth. Still, he was now twenty-five years old and was expected to marry. It was time for him to grow up, though he was still lacking a role model. Then something actually did happen to him—or rather, around him. He watched from his door on Court Street as an anti-abolitionist mob dragged the abolitionist publisher William Lloyd Garrison out of the office of his publication, the *Liberator*, and down the street when the sheriff intervened and carried Garrison to the safety of the jail. Twenty years later, Phillips recalled, "I was not in the street as one of the mob, but a spectator. I had come down from my office in Court Street to see what the excitement was. I did not understand anti-slavery then; that is, I did not understand the country in which I lived." But moved by that event (what Brahmin liked mobs?), he began to attend more closely to the abolitionist message.[14]

· · ·

In the 1830s, abolitionism was not yet a major force in American life, but Phillips gravitated toward it. "It was often a pleasant boast of Charles Sumner that he read the *Liberator* two years before I did," Phillips recalled. In the process, Phillips found himself on the fringe of a circle of women and men around Garrison, among them Ann Terry Greene. They fell in love. Two years younger than Phillips, Ann was the daughter of one of the wealthiest merchants in Boston, Benjamin Greene, and herself an abolitionist. Both her parents had died when she was a teenager, and she lived with her Weston cousins. She was not in good health, however, given to serious gastrointestinal and nervous disorders, and her condition fluctuated from fragile to deathly ill. She and Wendell had no children, and one may doubt whether their conjugal life was very active. Still, they remained married until Phillips's death in 1884. He was devoted to her, and she to him.[15]

The historian James Brewer Stewart has discovered in the Blagden papers (the family related to Ann's brothers) a trove of the couple's letters. They show that she missed him greatly when he went on speaking tours, and he was ridden with guilt about his absences. There was also the occasional substitution of the language of the nursery for the language of the marital bed. Was his traveling an attempt to escape Ann's control? Or to escape watching her deteriorate? Was his increasing vitriol on the podium an expression of frustration with his domestic situation? In any case, it was Ann and her circle who brought him fully into the movement, and to Garrison's side.[16]

· · ·

Modern abolitionism began in New England. It was perhaps unremark-
able that its spokesman was a man whose family status was fully equal to
Phillips's. Samuel Sewall was a well-to-do merchant and colonial judge
from a leading Massachusetts clan. His pamphlet *The Selling of Joseph*
(1700) laid out the core argument of the movement long before there was a
movement: "It is most certain that all Men, as they are the Sons of Adam,
are Coheirs; and have equal Right unto Liberty, and all other outward
Comforts of Life," for "Originally, and Naturally, there is no such thing
as Slavery. Joseph was rightfully no more a Slave to his Brethren, then
they were to him: and they had no more Authority to Sell him, than they
had to Slay him." From the first, then, the case against slavery was a legal one. During the Revolutionary Crisis, groups of the enslaved, aided by
Quakers, petitioned for an end to their bondage. One such petition from
1777, when the delegates to the state constitutional convention were de-
liberating, read, "[We understand] that [we] have, in common with all
other men, a natural & unalienable right to that freedom, which [God]
has [given] equally [to] all and which [we] have never [given up in] any
contract or agreement But [we] were unjustly dragged, by the cruel hand
of power, from [our] dearest friends, & some of [us] even torn from the
embraces of [our] tender parents . . . & brought [here] to be sold like
beasts of burden, & like them condemned to slavery for life—Every principle from which America has acted in the course of her unhappy difficulties
with Great-Britain, pleads stronger than a thousand arguments in favor of
[us]." In a series of cases in which putative enslavers were sued for assault
and battery (in attempting to recapture runaway enslaved people), juries
found the enslavers guilty. In 1783, Chief Justice Willian Cushing agreed
that slavery no longer existed in the state. Although the General Court
never passed a law ending slavery, it was assumed that Cushing's opinion
was sufficient to bar the institution. Some enslavers tried to retain their
bondsmen and -women by reclassifying them as indentured servants, thus
forcing those who refused to serve to win their freedom.[17]

Abolitionism gained ground in America during and after the Revolution. Laws in southern states made manumission easier. New Hampshire's constitution barred slavery, and New York and Pennsylvania passed
gradual emancipation laws. But the biggest gain came in the 1784 draft
for turning the Northwest Territory, gained from Britain, into new states.

Thomas Jefferson proposed that states carved out of the territory be free of slavery. This would protect the veterans of the war moving into the area from competing with the enslaved for work. The final version of the Northwest Ordinance passed into law in 1787, two months before the draft federal Constitution was submitted to Congress (for resubmission to the states for ratification). Article 6 of the Ordinance provided that "There shall be neither slavery nor involuntary servitude in the said territory, otherwise than in the punishment of crimes whereof the party shall have been duly convicted: Provided, always, That any person escaping into the same, from whom labor or service is lawfully claimed in any one of the original States, such fugitive may be lawfully reclaimed and conveyed to the person claiming his or her labor or service as aforesaid." Congress confirmed the bar on slavery in 1789. but made no provision for or against slavery in the southwestern lands between Georgia and the Mississippi. These soon became fertile fields for slavery and the internal slave trade.[18]

As slavery expanded geographically and in wealth, so did the potential for contention about slavery. Although antislavery agitation was not yet a major or ongoing preoccupation of American politicians, whenever the slavery issue did arise, as in the debate over the admission of Missouri as a slave state in 1820, it paralyzed Congress and resulted in sharp divisions, overheated rhetoric, and threats of dismemberment of the Union. "Yield nothing" was, for a time, the watchword of both sides in the lower house. In time, cooler heads prevailed in the Senate. As a result, the leaders of the major political parties agreed to a series of compromises designed less to resolve differences over slavery than to disguise the extent and consequences of those differences. Nevertheless, the Missouri Compromise left the nation holding "a wolf by the ear."[19]

The on-again, off-again consensus in the House of Representatives to avoid the slavery issue before 1832 collapsed when abolitionist agitation moved into a new and more strident phase. Earlier antislavery efforts entailed the purchase and relocation of formerly enslaved people to an African home by the American Colonization Society. The colonization plan was entirely voluntary, as was the gradual emancipation movement, which was intended to convince enslavers to free their bondsmen and-women. Neither of these movements made much headway in the Deep South, where forced labor was a vital part of staple-crop agriculture and the sale of surplus forced labor was a major source of income. In states such as South Carolina, even the whisper of emancipation led to public rebuke and the threat of violence.[20]

With the slavery issue throwing its shadow over national politics, on January 1, 1832, Garrison and other Massachusetts abolitionists founded the New England Anti-Slavery Society, a year after he had begun publication of the weekly antislavery newspaper the *Liberator*. In 1833, the society merged with others of the same persuasion as part of the American Anti-Slavery Society. The publicly declared goal of the society was the immediate end of slavery. The leadership rejected the gradualism of earlier abolitionist movements and denounced the project of sending the formerly enslaved back to Africa after buying them from their masters. The immediatist persuasion now had an institutional foundation and a potent voice.[21]

Garrison was a writer, however, not an orator. Phillips was often mentioned as Garrison's right-hand man in the abolitionist movement, but this is a little misleading. Garrison was agitating for the immediate end of slavery, beginning with his return to Boston from Baltimore in 1826. Garrison had his critics as well as his supporters, but he was the most visible of all the abolitionists until his death in 1879.[22]

Phillips did not convert to abolitionism because of his association with Garrison or the persuasive power of Garrison's advocacy, however. Phillips's biographer James Brewer Stewart opines that Phillips "hardly noticed" when a Boston mob chased Garrison through the streets. This not precisely true—it happened outside his office door. But there is no evidence that Phillips read the *Liberator* or attended abolitionist meetings until his courtship of Ann. She introduced him to Garrison, and soon Phillips was a habituate of her salon. The members of her circle were organizing antislavery petitions for Congress, which, led by southern members of the House, no longer accepted them starting in 1836. That was the second reason for Phillips's abolition conversion. Former president John Quincy Adams, sitting in Congress from Quincy, became the focal point of the so-called gag rule. Adams was much respected among the circle, although he was never an abolitionist. His increasingly vocal opposition to the gag rule nevertheless drew attention to it. A public meeting to discuss what Boston should do in response to the gag rule the next year prompted Phillips to speak out. And that speech brought him the attention that his law practice had not.[23]

·   ·   ·

Phillips's first major public speech came on March 28, 1837, in support of Adams's battle to read antislavery petitions in the House. Phillips spoke in Lynn, Massachusetts, at the Lyceum Theatre. Boston was a hotbed of proslavery mobbing, and no one was safe from these mobs in the streets. The motion was "*Resolved,* That the exertions of the Hon. John Quincy Adams, and the rest of the Massachusetts Delegation who sustained him, in his defence of the right of petition, deserve the cordial approbation and the gratitude of every American citizen."[24]

One must remember that Phillips was an avid newspaper reader. He included contemporary events in his speeches. No contemporary controversy was more important to the American Anti-Slavery Society than Adams's battle to read its petitions on the floor of the House. (They would then be recorded and published in the congressional *Register of Debates.*) Phillips, who loved early American history and honored the role of the Massachusetts men in the Revolution, knew that the right to petition the government for the redress of grievances was rooted in the Revolutionary Crisis and became a feature of state constitutions before it was enshrined in the Bill of Rights. The right of petition, along with the right to assemble peaceably and the right to speak and print free of prior censorship, had been tested in the Alien and Sedition Acts controversy of 1798–1800 and reaffirmed. They were a part of law that protected the people's access to lawmakers and a key element of what would become Phillips's own version of strong democratic positivism.[25]

Over the period from 1835 to 1836, anti-abolitionist violence had an unintended effect. The abolitionists found a different way to magnify their strength. New technologies in printing and the distribution of the mails suggested a change in tactics, moving the center of the project away from Boston to Washington, DC. That city, the home of the federal government and Congress, sat in the middle of slave country. Opposing slave auctions in the District, the abolitionists began to petition Congress for redress. Garrison did not originate this idea, but it struck him "like a thunderbolt." The petitions were not just a way of energizing a latent reformism. The thousands of signers could be regarded as a proxy electorate, because the petitions were sent to Congress. If they were read there, they would enter the public record and rouse public opinion.[26]

The District was (and is) governed by Congress. The theoretical question was whether Congress had the authority to end slavery there. A less comprehensive question was whether Congress could suppress the slave trade in the district. But in 1835 Washington, DC was a largely southern city in which slavery and the slave trade were legal and prospered. Public slave auctions reminded politicians from the free states how potent the slave lobby was, and the petitions raised that point. Many of these petitions, like letters to members of Congress today, were boilerplate—that is, they were preprinted, and the petitioners just had to fill in the blanks rather than writing individual letters. However, their propaganda value was not diminished by the anonymity of the petitioners.[27]

Phillips must have followed the events in Congress just as closely as Garrison's other supporters did. The newspapers had reporters at the sessions of the House to cover the debates there. What was more, the debates were summarized in the *Register of Debates* and its successor, the *Congressional Globe.*

When Phillips read about Adams pouring out his thoughts "before the people," he saw it as a forerunner of strong democratic positivism. When the Republicans won the presidency in 1860, Phillips returned to Adams's role in the gag rule debates. "The last ten years of JOHN QUINCY ADAMS were the frankest of his life. In them he poured out before the people the treason and the indignation which formerly he had only written in his diary."[28]

As the December 1835 session of the Twenty-Fourth Congress opened, the slavery issue that had long lurked in the corridors of the Capitol entered its legislative chambers. The first business of December 16 was the reading of petitions. James Fairfield, representing York County, Maine, rose to present a petition from 172 ladies of the county begging Congress to end slavery in the District. Two days later, James Henry Hammond of South Carolina responded with a novel proposal. Previously, antislavery petitions had been summarily laid on the table or referred to the committee on the District, where they would die a slow death. He wanted the House to go further by rejecting them outright as an insult to the honor of the South.[29]

As a gentleman, Phillips understood honor as not just reputation but more important, what a man thought of himself. Hammond's concept of honor was almost diametrically opposed. To Hammond, honor was what others thought of the man. He and those who later supported his resolution called the abolitionists bloodthirsty creatures who would set the enslaved on their masters. No southern woman or child—he did not say, but he implied, white woman or child—would be safe from the innately savage Africans if they were freed from their bondage (or if they had access to abolitionist writings). Hammond judged that it was necessary to "put a more decided seal of reprobation" on the petitions. His proposal was seconded by Virginia's John Mercer Patton, who said that he wished to quiet the anxiety raised by the reading of the petitions. Patton's was a second and less confrontational strand in the argument for the gag rule. His anxiety was shared by his fellow southern members and presumably the white citizens of his District.[30]

On the 23rd of the month, the Vermont congressman William Slade raised the stakes. He not only read another petition but urged (as Fairfield had not) Congress to answer the pleas of his petitioners. In the course of his remarks, he mentioned the "evils of slavery" and called the petition one which Congress must consider. Two days later, after the attempted reading of yet another petition, Hammond moved that it and all such petitions should not be received at all.[31]

Responding to another spate of antislavery petitions arriving at the next meeting of Congress, in February 1836, Hammond again called for a blanket rejection of all antislavery petitions. He made clear his objections to the petitions, though he conceded his "sacred regard for the inestimable right of petition," but argued Congress's refusal to receive such petitions did not deny anyone's right to petition. It was a clever point and might have closed the debate with a whimper, but Hammond could not restrain himself. Once again, he did just what the petitioners wanted—he made slavery itself the focus of the debate.[32]

Convoyed by a flotilla of similar speeches, the South Carolina initiative to reject the petitions sailed ahead. Various plans for silencing the petitioners were referred to a special committee headed by South Carolina's Henry L. Pinckney, underlining the special interest that South Carolina had in the outcome. The committee and then the House struggled over how to phrase the committee resolution: should it reject, refer, or table the petitions? Should it include a condemnation of the petitioners? At first, the resolution ended with a sop to the North—an afterthought that the petitioners were not necessarily evil men and women. Even this palliative was unacceptable to Hammond and his allies. It was removed from the final version of the Pinckney committee resolution of May 1836. The result was a vote on May 26, 1836, not to receive any of the petitions.[33]

Led by Senator John C. Calhoun, the upper house would adopt a parallel policy to the House's gag rule. Each petition would be received and then automatically referred to committee, forestalling antislavery senators from making speeches in support of the petition. As was customary in the Senate, the procedure did not have to be renewed at the start of each session.[34]

The gag rule debates, however, had awakened a sleeping tiger—John Quincy Adams. He saw a threat to freedom of speech, press, and petition. Adams, to whom a number of the petitions had been sent directly, now wanted to know if Congress had gagged him. It would seem, at first glance, that nothing could be further from the grassroots radical abolitionist movement than the privilege of freedom of speech that an elite public figure claimed in Congress. The connection was clear in hindsight, however. It was the free speech of the abolitionists that opponents in both the North and the South threatened. The mobs that disrupted abolitionist meetings in Philadelphia, Boston, and elsewhere in free states and burned abolitionist literature in slave states violently denied the rights of the abolitionists. Forcibly driving abolitionists from meeting halls and breaking into post offices to seize and destroy abolitionist writings were commonplace and even praised by southern members of Congress. In 1836, Senator Thomas Hart Benton of Missouri praised the mobs for "silencing the gabbling tongues of female dupes and disper[sing] the assemblies" of the abolitionist "fanatics and visionaries." He did not mention the First Amendment. In response, "free speech became a rallying cry" for the abolitionists. As the American Anti-Slavery Society executive board announced in 1835, "We never intend to surrender the liberty of press, of speech, or of conscience." Adams's high dudgeon on the floor of the House might reflect his sense of his own importance rather than genuine camaraderie with the abolitionists, but the gag rule debates brought them together.[35]

Adams's motives in entering the debate, indeed in becoming its storm center, may never be fully understood. A man of almost rigid integrity, he kept public displays of his emotions to a minimum, though his diary reveals a man of passionate and strident opinions. The former fifth president of the United States, whose return to public life as a congressman from Massachusetts had made him an elder statesman of the Republic, he was one of the few remaining links to the generation of the founders. As ambassador to Russia and later as Secretary of State, he had argued with great force and ingenuity for Britain to pay enslavers for the bondmen the Royal Navy had carried away after the War of 1812. Even then, he had conceded, "Certainly a living, sentient being, and still more a human being, was to be regarded in a different light from the inanimate matter of which other private property might consist." Adams was not an abolitionist. Indeed, he viewed the rise of the abolitionist movement with a certain realistic detachment. He thought slavery an abomination, but he had little use for radical abolitionist plans. Over the course of the gag rule debates, he would express his antislavery views with stronger and stronger language. Whether that shift was rooted in his animosity toward the Jacksonian Democrats of the South or the evolution of his views on slavery, historians disagree.[36]

Though painfully aware of the debilities he had acquired over his nearly seventy years of active service for his country, Adams was especially concerned that the voices of his fellow New Englanders might be muzzled by Hammond's resolution. He was not a power broker in the Whig Party; indeed, he stood apart from (and he believed himself above) the conflict between the Democratic and Whig Parties. But privately and then publicly he began a campaign against the gag rule as an unconstitutional imposition on the rights of citizens and their representatives. With the gag rule debate emerging, he confided to his diary on the 26th of December, 1835: "Harassed excessively with my own reflections upon the proposed new rule for the transaction of business in the House, upon which I grow disheartened as I proceed, and consider what I ought to say, but what it will probably be of no avail if I do say it. My mind is oppressed beyond what it ever was before, between a sense of public duty to take a bold and independent stand, and the almost certainty of being overpowered and broken down in the operation."[37]

When the House once again sat, on the 12th of January, 1836, Adams was still unsure of what to do. Fearing that no action on his part would suffice and, seeing all manner of evils from every action, he elected a middle course. "As the petitioners had thought proper to send their petition to me, I wished to be able to inform them what disposition of it has been made by the House."[38]

For a time, Adams could not take any real part in the debate—swelling in his legs prevented him from attending Congress. He returned to find the issue tucked away in the Pinckney committee. When Adams attempted to enter the discussion, the Speaker of the House, James K. Polk of Tennessee,

Jackson's protégé, refused to give Adams the floor. Adams waited with increasing frustration as the House voted to excise the last part of the resolution (finding the petitioners to be decent folk). "I rose . . . but I was called with great vociferation to order, and not permitted to proceed."[39]

At first, Adams tried a procedural approach, engaging in a running commentary with the Speaker and other members on House rules past and present. Nothing could fully silence Adams's voice on the floor, even if he had to shout over other members' voices. Adams lost his patience. The resolution was unconstitutional, he shouted from his desk but to no effect. Was he gagged? he continued, giving the rule its popular name. No one answered. He then commenced a guerilla war against the gag rule. He questioned the accuracy of the clerk Walter Franklin's record of the vote on the resolution. It seemed to be 117 in favor and 68 against, but two members, Henry Wise of Virginia and Thomas Glascock of Georgia, had refused to vote on it. Adams insisted that the record reflect their refusal, rather than simply note that they had not voted. As a result, the rest of May 26 was taken up with Speaker Polk, Adams, Wise, and Glascock going over the previous day's events. "Great disorder ensued," the clerk noted as he valiantly tried to record their conversation. He had to put it in the record, lest Adams once again challenge its accuracy. This awkward merry-go-round was Adams's way of prolonging debate on the resolution by proxy after Representative Owens and Speaker Polk refused to let him speak directly about the resolution itself.[40]

On December 26, 1836, Adams tried to introduce a petition against slavery in the District. Rep. Francis Pickens, a future governor of Confederate South Carolina, objected. Had not the issue been decided in May? Polk, still sitting in the Speaker's chair, ruled that the Pinckney resolution vote no longer bound the members. When Adams's attempt to read the petition was nevertheless objected to, he responded that "it appeared to him that the decision of the House at the last session went quite far enough to suppress the right of petition of the citizens of this country, and quite far enough to suppress the freedom of speech." But the motion not to receive any petition "went one step further. It went to settle the principle that petitions . . . should not even be received, and that, too, directly in the face of the Constitution itself." Adams's focus remained on the constitutional question. The rights he defended were not those of the enslaved but of the free petitioners. "He hoped the people of this country would not tamely submit to the injustice and wrong which would be inflicted upon them by their immediate representatives, in deciding that their petitions should not be received."[41]

On March 7, 1837, the newly elected Democratic president, Martin Van Buren, addressed the attendees at his inaugural. He referred to the gag rule issue indirectly, warning against those in or out of government undermining "domestic institutions which, unwisely disturbed, might endanger the harmony of the whole." It was clear to all what he meant. But if high-sounding generality would not suffice, he made the point even clearer by repeating a portion of the letter he had sent to the House in the spring of 1836. Van Buren recognized the dangers of bringing the slavery debate to the center of national politics. Sectional discord could easily lead to the breakup of a union of free and slave states. "The last, perhaps the greatest, of the prominent sources of discord and disaster supposed to lurk in our political condition was the institution of domestic slavery." Van Buren then essayed a form of policy analysis that would become a commonplace of American political rhetoric—the appeal to the founders. "Our forefathers were deeply impressed with the delicacy of this subject, and they treated it with a forbearance so evidently wise that in spite of every sinister foreboding it never until the present period disturbed the tranquility of our common country." As a rhetorical device, the appeal was effective. As history, it was nonsense. Disagreements over slavery had erupted during the Constitutional Convention, paralyzed Congress in the Missouri statehood controversy, and had reappeared over the question of the annexation of the new Republic of Texas. Van Buren knew the lesson he wanted to derive from history, however, and facts were not going to deter him. "Such a result is sufficient evidence of the justice and the patriotism of their course; it is evidence not to be mistaken that an adherence to it can prevent all embarrassment from this as well as from every other anticipated cause of difficulty or danger." Van Buren realized that the only way to win the highest office was to get votes from both North and South. Indeed, the political party system of the period insured that presidential candidates were as appealing to as many voters as possible.[42]

. . .

Aware of all this controversy—more, inflamed by it—absorbing every detail from the newspapers, perhaps, one wonders, seeing himself as a younger version of Adams, Phillips was primed to make his maiden appearance on the issue. Thus, the first public address Phillips gave came not in the early 1830s in support of Garrison but later on the gag rule question. On March 28, 1837, at the Anti-Slavery Society of Lynn, Massachusetts, Phillips addressed himself to the resolution before the body: thanks to John Quincy Adams for his opposition to the gag rule. It is important to note that Phillips was not speaking as a die-hard abolitionist, but as an advocate of freedom of speech. That was Adams's posture as well. How better to introduce strong democratic positivism than by defending the established rights of petition and speech? The essence of strong democratic positivism was that the law must be obeyed because everyone had a chance to participate in lawmaking. Thus, Adams's "course during the last session deserves the gratitude of every American; for in that contest, he was not the representative of any State or any party, but the champion of the fundamental principles of the Constitution." From the first, the focus of Phillips's address was Adams's own focus—that the question was one of constitutional rights abused by the defenders of slavery. The appeal was not only to the law in the abstract, but to the civil magistracy. "We had heard, at a time of profound peace, in the midst of our most crowded cities, the voice of the multitude once and again overwhelmed the voice of the laws, almost without the shadow of an attempt at resistance on the part of the civil magistrate." Adams spoke for no party; no interest of his was invaded; he had nothing to gain for his friends, and he was wary of the abolitionists' persistence but "statesman-like, he saw the end from the beginning. When rights were invaded, he was willing to side with any who rallied to protect them." At the very end of the address, Phillips recalled himself to the subject of the society: "But I will not wander from my subject to slavery; it is our own rights which are at issue; and the first cry that awakened the nation to the importance of that issue, was the voice of the Ex-President." The issue of slavery, to Phillips at least, was inseparable from the issue of free persons' legal rights.[43]

If Phillips's intervention in the gag rule meeting resembled Adams's own style—high minded, above party and faction, and rooted in a profound respect for the Constitution and the political institutions it created—in short, patrician officeholding. But Phillips did not hold office. His advocacy was free of party taint because he did not belong to a party. He did not condemn Congress or anyone in a law-making capacity. He merely argued for obedience to law—the Bill of Rights. "It is our own rights" which were at stake.

Law, properly seen, was the command of the state reified in the voice of the people. What was more, it rested on the importance of the people's access to their government. It was democratic. Thus, Phillips's nascent jurisprudence of strong democratic positivism was born before he adopted the role of public interest lawyer. But that role would soon come.

. . .

By the end of 1837, with such appeals to strong democratic positivism having no impact on the underlying issue of slavery or its advocates, Phillips reappeared in the public arena with a very different theory of government. It was also his first public interest lawyering intervention in response to a nation roiling in anti-abolitionist violence. Phillips spoke during a debate at Faneuil Hall on December 8, 1837, over a resolution condemning an anti-abolitionist mob for the murder of the abolitionist preacher and printer Elijah P. Lovejoy earlier that year. Like many other lower-middle-class New Englanders, Lovejoy moved about the Northeast and Midwest, seeking a sense of purpose and a calling. He was drawn to cities, and at times was a printer, a teacher, a minister, and last an abolitionist publicist. In 1836, he moved his press from St. Louis in slave-state Missouri—a hotbed of proslavery activity and, at the same time, of abolitionist agitation—to Alton in free-state Illinois, across the Mississippi River and supposedly greater safety. But Lovejoy's reputation as a relentless crusader preceded him. A year later, in 1837, the warehouse where he kept his press was once again attacked by a proslavery mob, and this time defended by twelve of his supporters. When the attackers hurled rocks and placed a ladder on the side of the building, Lovejoy, inside with the others, volunteered to step outside and confront the mob. He was immediately shot dead. It was a shot that roused the abolitionists, the *Liberator* printing the news in an issue with a black border. Phillips recalled, many years later, "I can never forget the quick, sharp, agony of that hour which brought us news of Lovejoy's death." It was for young Abraham Lincoln an alarm bell, indicating how deadly the conflict with proslavery forces in the North had become. It was for Phillips a wake-up call, and it changed the way he viewed opposition to abolition. Thus the gag rule debate that was unfolding before him was the precipitating event for Phillips's transformation into the first public interest lawyer.[44]

The meeting after the death of Lovejoy was called to order by Jonathan Phillips (a cousin of Wendell). The resolutions, read by Benjamin

Hallett, condemned the violence at Alton. The Massachusetts attorney general, James T. Austin, attended although he was not a member of the group. Austin was speaking only for himself, not as a representative of the Massachusetts government. Arguing against any support for Lovejoy, he compared the anti-abolitionist mob to the patriots of 1776. Calling out from the audience, he opined that Lovejoy had been a fool who had died a fool's death. Phillips was also in the audience and rushed to the podium to disagree. Austin was trying to gag the meeting, but Phillips was not about to let that happen. Speaking without notes, he fumed, "The mob at Alton were met to wrest from a citizen his just rights,—met to resist the laws. . . . He was not only defending the freedom of the press, but he was under his own roof . . . with the sanction of the civil authority. The men who assailed him went against and over the laws." Phillips was lecturing Austin, who should have known better. Although they were not in court, they argued the point as two lawyers—but Phillips had the better argument, based on positivist principles. John Austin (no relation to James Austin) had already explained that the law was the command of the state and must be obeyed. Phillips did not question the mandate of state law or call for violating it, but he read Massachusetts Revolutionary history differently from Austin. To him, Lovejoy's actions were like those of the patriots, protesting within the law against the injustice of the Crown and its lawyers.[45]

Lovejoy, as Phillips conceived of him, did not violate the laws but embodied them. Lovejoy had stood on his constitutional rights to speak and to print. The mob trampled on those rights when they killed him. Phillips knew that he was arguing against the state attorney general, whose elite credentials were as well established as his own, and admitted that he himself had never "been heard" in the Hall, but youth should not discredit what he said, for his was the better interpretation of law. In fact, the meeting had convened in the courtroom of the statehouse, and in effect Phillips acted the part of counsel arguing a case against the state. Lovejoy was not a criminal but was merely protecting his property. "The question now is, Did he act within the Constitution and the laws ?" Lovejoy, like Phillips himself, acted within the law and with its sanction. The anti-abolitionist mob acted outside the law. "But all you who believe, as I do, in the right and duty of magistrates to execute the laws" saw the hypocrisy in men like Austin, who refused law in aid of the abolitionists' rights. "This clerical absurdity chooses as a check for the abuses of the press, not the law but the dread of a mob. By so doing, it deprives not only the individual and the minority of their rights, but the majority also, since the expression of their opinion may sometimes provoke disturbance from the minority." The hecklers' veto had replaced the right to assemble, speak and print. At its inception, then, Phillips's positivism—the laws that protected free speech, the press, and petition, must be obeyed—fit easily with his abolitionism. But the logic of his positivism was already leading him to a very different place.[46]

. . .

Phillips knew the risks he was taking in his open advocacy of abolition. But his feet felt on surer ground each time he stood at the lectern. He sensed the power of the spoken word, even when actions—like Lovejoy's— could be dangerous. No help came from mainstream politics. Both the Democratic and the Whig parties spurned abolitionism. Even those politicians who were antislavery, like the young William Henry Seward, did not advocate an immediate end to the institution. How then were a handful of journalists, teachers, preachers, and lawyers to bring the slave machinery to a halt? The answer seemed clear to Phillips: unrelenting, unforgiving public advocacy. If the politicians would not listen, perhaps the people would. He was beginning to see a source of law beyond statutes and constitutions. That source was the people. His positivism was increasingly populist. But popular opinion faced an obstacle: slavery was legal.

From New York, where a rival antislavery society to Garrison's had appeared, came one possible solution to the problem of slave law. Alvan Stewart, an Upstate New York abolitionist, had already proposed it in 1836. In his "Answer to the Message of Governor Marcy [of New York]," Stewart insisted that "since 1808, that institution [the Constitution] is free from the imputation of sustaining slavery." Repeatedly thereafter, he made the same claim, basing it on the proposition that the framers had intended to abolish slavery. He found evidence for it in the Preamble to the Constitution and in the Fifth Amendment. A practicing lawyer in the New York courts with a unique courtroom demeanor, a gift for irony, and a reputation for wit, Stewart was one of the "radical abolitionists" of the 1830s and a founder of the New York Anti-Slavery Society. He was also a popular orator; his speech before the New Jersey Anti-Slavery Society, in which he argued for an antislavery Constitution, combined passionate moral and religious beliefs with oratorical skills. He was not the most logical of thinkers, however, and his argument that the Constitution was innately antislavery was more a claim than a reasoned argument. In any case, it was too soon in the course of the movement for that idea to have much traction. His energies then went to the founding of the Liberty Party. He died in 1849.[47]

Phillips knew about Stewart, but he was skeptical about the argument that the Constitution was antislavery. He certainly did not include it in his repertoire of public addresses. Instead, he was creeping toward the opposite position, that the Constitution and the Union it created were so thoroughly attached to slavery that the only legal remedy for abolitionists was to leave the Union. But that extreme stance would require two more catalysts. The first was the rise of a political movement (in which Stewart had a part) to legislate the end of slavery. The second was the question of annexing Texas.

In the meantime, lecturing as a profession had gained popularity during the first four decades of the century. Phillips's fellow New Englanders, for example, Ralph Waldo Emerson, went about giving lectures for fees. The lyceum movement of evening lectures spread from New England throughout the country. Some could make a nice living doing this, and that is what Phillips decided to do. Like the Great Awakening's George Whitefield and Jonathan Edwards in the mid-eighteenth century, and Charles Grandison Finney in his own time, Phillips went on the circuit. There he found a proxy for the people as a whole in voluntary gatherings of interested listeners. But the time did not seem ripe for a political conversion to match the period's religious revivalism, and instead of friendly audiences of like-minded people, Phillips often found himself among skeptics and critics.[48]

CHAPTER 2

Agitator

*B*y the beginning of the 1840s, Phillips had committed himself to the role of antislavery agitator, speaking whenever and wherever he could against the institution of slavery. But it seemed that his words made little headway against the winds of events, although his talks drew large audiences, and his words were widely reported.

By the end of the 1830s, the spread of slavery in the United States seemed unstoppable. The "peculiar institution" blossomed as Alabama, Mississippi, and Arkansas entered the Union as slave states. Enslavers who had carried their bondsmen into Tejas in the 1820s demanded annexation by the United States in 1835. Antislavery leaders in Congress feared that annexation would bring four new slave states into the Union. John Quincy Adams and a handful of determined congressmen joined with Free Soilers (opponents of the expansion of slavery) and abolitionists to resist. The New York abolitionist Alvan Stewart persuaded Kentucky's James G. Birney and a handful of others to form a new national party, the Liberty Party. Birney ran as its presidential candidate in 1840 but won few votes. Although the party continued to exist until 1860, it had far less impact than its successor, the Free Soil Party of 1848. Abolition in the United States was still a relatively small movement.[1]

• • •

A different story played out across the Atlantic and in the other colonies of Great Britain. Although slavery in the United States would not have been possible without slavery in the British Empire—the British economy depended in part on the products of slave labor and the empire profited from the Atlantic slave trade—at the end of the eighteenth century and with greater impetus into the new century, a movement for emancipation grew in Britain. When the North American colonies won their independence, one economic benefit to England from slavery weakened. The rise of the American cotton supply still tied British mills to American plantations, and slavery remained the primary labor system in the British sugar islands, but the attack on the overseas slave trade in Britain became an attack on slavery in its overseas possessions. British laboring interests joined with reform movements to call for the end of slavery throughout the British Empire. It helped the cause that slavery had no foothold in the home islands. By the early 1830s, the demand had grown so strong that Parliament considered a gradual abolition, and the Slavery Abolition (Emancipation) Act of 1833 treated former slaves as apprentices to their former masters. This satisfied no one—not the formerly enslaved, nor their enslavers, nor the reformers at home. In 1838 the experiment in apprenticeship ended, and the enslaved were freed unconditionally. But freedom was not an entire success, as the white landowners in the Caribbean expected the newly freed to work long hours under harsh conditions.[2]

In part for Ann's health, Wendell and Ann Phillips traveled to Europe in 1840. In London, they attended the June 1840 meeting of the World Anti-Slavery Convention. Phillips was a delegate, but he and Ann encountered controversy from the moment they tried to take their seats. The convention organizers originally had barred women; British Victorian mores excluded women from public life (ironic in light of the gender of the British sovereign). Among the Massachusetts and Pennsylvania delegations were women who would later play a leading role in the first wave of feminist reform, including Elizabeth Cady Stanton and Lucretia Mott. Phillips protested, and women were seated separately from men but not permitted to address the delegates. Garrison, among others, chose to sit with the women. Stanton and Mott left London after the first day of the meeting, convinced that women needed their own emancipation movement.[3]

On July 6, 1840, two weeks after the close of the convention, Phillips spoke to the British India Society. He was their inaugural speaker, and his subject was cotton. In the United States, the 1830s had brimmed over with what contemporary reformers called "freedom's ferment." Movements for the reform of insane asylums, prisons, public education, temperance, and even free love had made their presence felt. Nascent socialist experiments in New Jersey and Indiana had appeared. But the antislavery movement had stalled. Phillips exaggerated when he said that ten years earlier, the founders of the New England Anti-Slavery Society thought that their task would be easy. They had only to convince the enslavers that free labor was more efficient and economical than slave labor. Phillips opined, "It would be safe; it would be just": in a liberty-loving country, surely the enslavers would see the light. But ten years of resistance in the South and violence in the North had convinced the abolitionists that the way ahead was anything but easy. But now the prospect of cotton production in India had given the abolitionists, and the enslaved, new hope. Surely with their British textile market for raw cotton gone, the institution of slavery would follow. How could American slavery "stand against" the vast reaches of Indian lands and the numbers of willing free laborers growing cotton? For if "slavery [could] only be maintained by monopoly," end that monopoly, and the economics of slavery would dictate what humane pleading could not accomplish, for the "only voice" that the American cotton nabobs heard was the voice of profits; still that voice, and the job was done. A final admonition: "Take care that in driving our cotton from your shores you do not admit a single pound that is blood-stained from ours." But they did, for Britain's textile mills were voracious consumers of American cotton. And that was not the whole of the story, for the textile miles of Massachusetts and Pennsylvania gorged themselves on southern cotton as well and in turn sold clothing to the enslavers for the enslaved.[4]

Phillips was not alone in trying to predict the course of cotton production and its labor force. In 1858, James Henry Hammond, returned to the Senate from South Carolina, would explain how the expansion of slavery was inevitable, because "cotton is king." Indian cotton production did not and would not dampen northern textile mills' demand for the raw product. Slavery and cotton would make the South the center of an American empire, Hammond declared, for "in this territory lies the great valley of the Mississippi, now the real, and soon to be the acknowledged seat of the empire of the world. The sway of that valley will be as great as ever the Nile knew in the earlier ages of mankind. We own the most of it. The most valuable part of it belongs to us now; and although those who have settled above us are now opposed to us, another generation will tell a different tale. They are ours by all the laws of nature; slave-labor will go over every foot of this great valley where it will be found profitable to use it, and some of those who may not use it are soon to be united with us by such ties as will make us one and inseparable." American economic progress rested on southern staple exports. As it happened, there was much truth to that lower-level causal thesis.[5]

.   .   .

In 1841, Wendell and Ann Phillips returned to Boston, and Phillips immersed himself in struggles against racism close to home. He began to ride the rails, literally, joining Black abolitionists in the rail cars reserved for people of color. They were disgusting. "Dirt cars," the abolitionist riders called them, and they insisted that their two-dollar tickets entitled them to ride in the white cars. On February 10, 1842, Phillips testified before a committee of the Massachusetts legislature that the Eastern Rail Road and other rail companies that segregated people of color violated the state's constitution. The solution was a simple one: "we ask the legislature to say what is law," because even private corporations traveled on right of way gained from public domain and relied on public law. A new law forbidding public transportation to discriminate on the basis of race was not needed—simply enforce the state constitution. The testimony did not change matters, but continued direct action by riders did. Segregation on the public carriers ended the next year.[6]

Phillips later joined in the battle against segregated schools in Boston. The school board had segregated the schools, and the city solicitor, Peleg Chandler, had explained why segregation was good for all parties. The abolitionist Henry W. Bowditch prepared a reply. It bore the marks of the antislavery bar to which he belonged. He supposed that the state was the primary source "of all political authority" and rested upon the will of the people. But that will could not impose injustice on any portion of the people because of their alleged particular conditions. The separate schools were inferior, and segregation of children into them was a distinction that the state constitution barred. Phillips added his own views, which were far more pointed. Along the way, he called out the educator Horace Mann for his "timid silence." The city solicitor and the board did not see that "such a system of schools is illegal and unreasonable in the legal sense of the word."

Were there a legal basis for discrimination in the public schools, one would find the same discrimination in all the public laws. But that was not the case, because the state constitution had explicitly forbidden such distinctions. If this exception to the general law was permissible, then it had to be explicit in the state constitution. It was not. Nor was the school board given such discretion. That would have been an impermissible delegation of the power belonging to the people as a whole. (Phillips did conclude that "in his heart," Chandler opposed the caste schools—perhaps because Chandler was notably deaf and had to use an ear trumpet a yard long to engage in legal business.) Like Phillips's testimony in the railroad case, this was excellent lawyering. The board was not swayed, however, and when its decision was tested in the state's highest court, Chief Justice Lemuel Shaw found that any prejudice in the policy was not created by the law and could not be changed by changing the law. The segregated school system remained—briefly. In part because of Phillips's pleading before the court of public opinion, the state legislature again changed the law a year later.[7]

In both segregation cases, Phillips acted in the role of public interest lawyer. He did not have a formal (paying) client. (He did not need clients; with his own inherited wealth and Ann's wealth, he was one of the richest men in Boston.) He intervened because he believed in the cause of desegregation. Addressing public bodies, he spoke in terms of best public outcomes. Characteristically, he did not confine himself to legal issues, however, but ranged over religious, political, and social matters. He did not pull his punches. In asides, he condemned the recently deceased Supreme Court Justice Joseph Story for his opinion in *Prigg v. Pennsylvania*. He slammed Horace Mann. Both were leading figures in Massachusetts law and education, respectively, and there was no reason for Phillips to mention them, much less denigrate them. But they had failed to live up to his expectations, and more important, had failed (in his opinion) to uphold the law. Of Mann: he had a duty to all students, regardless of race. Of Story, Phillips railed that "when a man puts on the robes of office, his acts become the property of the nation." Phillips had merely "summoned" Story "to the bar of public opinion." If the law was to be obeyed, it must treat persons equally.[8]

.   .   .

The doctrine Phillips defended was his own version of strong democratic positivism. But in the years between the two segregation cases, he (along with Garrison) was developing a far more radical position on positivism that his attack on Story and Mann reflected. Phillips never argued that the Massachusetts state constitution must be voided, but the logic of his anti-slavery argument led him to an extreme position—he called for dissolution of the federal Union and the rewriting of the federal Constitution to bar slavery. Recall that officials swear to preserve and defend the Constitution, not the Union. Phillips could have made this distinction and still taken the oath, but nowhere did he split this hair. If the existence of the Union enabled slavery, and if the free states' continued participation in national politics legitimated slave states' laws, and if the Constitution allowed slave states to exist in the Union, then the free states must leave it. He stated this proposition throughout the 1840s and 1850s, beginning with his abolitionist speeches in 1842. "The union of liberty and slavery, in one just and equal and compact, is that which it is not in the power of God and men to achieve. . . . And therefore the American Union is such only in form, but not in substance, a hollow mockery." It was a short step from that to conclude that the Union must be dissolved, and the Constitution rewritten. William Lloyd Garrison, editor of the *Liberator*, agreed with Phillips. The newspaper regularly published both men's calls for the end of the Union. Indeed, soon it was impossible to separate the language of the two men on the subject. But Phillips's method for severing the connection, unlike Garrison's, was through law. Let Congress do it, Phillips insisted. This was another inconsistency, but by this time, consistency was not his aim.[9]

Perhaps the signal event seconding Phillips's rejection of the federal Constitution was the arrest of the enslaved runaway George Latimer of Virginia, in Boston in October 1842. It set loose the fury of the abolitionists, and none was more furious than Phillips. Justice Joseph Story, sitting with the federal circuit court, had ordered Latimer's detention on the basis of the federal Fugitive Slave Act of 1793, passed to give effect to the Rendition Clause in Article IV of the Constitution. This law gave federal officers the authority to hold, detain, and hand over suspected runaways to slave catchers. (This was no doubt one reason that Phillips in 1846 would accuse Story of violating the law.) Latimer's freedom was less the issue than the power of the Virginia slave system to reach into free Massachusetts and pluck out one of its residents. While Latimer sat in jail and his putative owner, Edward Mallery, arranged for his bondsman's return to slavery, the abolitionists rented Faneuil Hall to protest. Phillips's fury outran his good sense, and he railed that "my curse be on the Constitution of the United States." Although he and Garrison had already decided that the existing frame of government was a covenant with death, shouting that admonition to a surging crowd in a public meeting was a little different from publishing it in a journal that had a limited circulation among friends of the movement.[10]

As a matter of law, Phillips's view was an entirely different proposition from Vice President John C. Calhoun's 1828 justification of secession. In the infamous, secretly authored defense of South Carolina's Nullification Proclamation, Calhoun argued that the Union was created as a compact among sovereign states, with the Constitution spelling out the terms of that compact. When the federal government violated the terms of that compact, any state, of its own volition, might leave the Union. Phillips never accepted the compact theory of the Union. His target was the Constitution itself, and his solution was to dissolve the Union. In page after page of the *Liberator* throughout the 1840s, he repeated this position— the Constitution was a pact with the devil, and the federal government was the devil's agent. It followed that no righteous citizen (that is, no abolitionist) should vote, for a vote implied support for the "whole of the" Constitution. He had abandoned John Quincy Adams' constitutionalist posture for a far more radical stance.[11]

. . .

The looming Texas annexation question had convinced Phillips that an examination of the Constitution's support of slavery was long overdue. Phillips's collection of documents on the Constitution, published in 1844, has never been given the attention it deserves. Madison's notes on the debates at the Constitutional Convention had at last been published as volumes 2 and 3 of *The Papers of James Madison* (1840). Phillips's gloss on these was a genuine contribution to constitutional discourse, anticipating the modern elevation of Madison to the first rank in constitutional thought. Filling nearly 250 pages, Phillips's gloss became part of the national conversation over the gag rule debates and the impending Texas annexation. The extensive collection of documents, including Madison's notes, the speeches of leading figures at the Constitutional Convention, and the ratification debates in various states proved that a compromise had been reached on slavery. Phillips summarized it as "granting to the slaveholder distinct privileges and protection for his slave property, in return for certain commercial concessions on his part toward the North. They prove also that the nation at large was fully aware of this bargain at the time and entered into it willingly and with open eyes." He stated his purpose in such clear fashion that it should have gained far more attention then (and now) than it did. "We do not produce the extracts which make up these pages to show what is the meaning of the clauses above cited. For no man or party of any authority in such matters has ever pretended to doubt to what subject they all relate." Phillips had adopted a bold, simple, public original-meaning jurisprudence.[12]

Originalism, or original meaning, was not then, as it is now, a leading interpretive school. The notion that the constitutional text should be read in light of its framers' intent made perfect sense, however, to a generation that knew and revered the framers. They had been a living source of meaning. But the framers had dodged the question of slavery, omitting the word itself from the text while agreeing to a number of proslavery compromises. These were the three-fifths clause for representation of states in the lower house (including three fifths of "other persons" in the count); the Rendition Clause, mandating the return to the state of origin of those held to labor in those states; and the nonimportation clause, barring Congress from prohibiting the "importation" of persons until 1808. Given these contradictions, an originalist interpretation of slavery in the Constitution still does not produce incontrovertible results.[13]

Phillips's denunciation of the Constitution did not mean he had ceased to think and speak like a lawyer. He continued to practice, after a fashion, working with his younger brother Grenville. He still lectured, however. He repeated some of these lectures all over the Northeast. But his antislavery orations were of a different and more fervent sort. He explained, "I obey those laws which seem to me good, because they are good—and I submit to all the penalties which my disobedience of the rest brings on me." He accepted the authority of the Supreme Court when it upheld the supremacy of federal law regarding enslaved runaways. His logic was unassailable, he thought. The (to him) proslavery Constitution was the law of the land. What he refused to accept was that a political solution to the slavery problem was possible. Thus the course of politics in the 1840s both fulfilled his direst predictions (slavery had both government and law on its side) and horrified him. He rejected the overtures of the new Liberty Party and shunned the proposals of the subsequent Free-Soilers.[14]

For more moderate opponents of slavery than Phillips, Garrison, and their cadre, the key political issue was not the elimination of slavery—that was not likely in the near future—but confining slavery to the places where it already existed. The successor to the Liberty Party was the Free Soil movement. Not everyone in that political faction believed in the equality of persons, however. Free-Soilers simply argued that slavery was wrong and should not be allowed to enlarge itself. Worse, slavery undermined free labor, and free labor was the moral center of the movement. Free labor as a concept had a longer and more complex pedigree than antislavery. Labor gave dignity to free men. Anything that diminished the space that free labor occupied was anathema to the Free-Soilers.[15]

. . .

The origins of the Free Soil movement lay in the effort by proslavery politicians to annex Texas. In 1841 Virginia's John Tyler became president on the sudden death of the Whig William Henry Harrison. Tyler was a Democrat, and along with much of his party, wanted to expand the nation to the west. The southern Democrats saw the application of the Republic of Texas to join the United States as an opportunity to wed westward expansion to the expansion of slavery. Other members of the Democratic Party, along with northern "Conscience" (antislavery) Whigs, opposed annexation, wishing to keep slavery out of the national political arena. They were aware that the debate over the admission of Missouri as a slave state had brought Congress to its knees with threats of secession and violence.[16]

Nonetheless, in April 1844, Secretary of State John C. Calhoun negotiated a treaty with Texas providing for the annexation of that country. Henry Clay and Martin Van Buren, the two front-runners for the major party presidential nominations in the 1844 election, both announced their opposition to annexation, and the Senate blocked the treaty. To the surprise of Clay and other Whigs, the 1844 Democratic National Convention rejected Van Buren in favor of James K. Polk and approved a platform calling for the acquisition of both Texas and the Oregon territory. Polk went on to defeat Clay in a close election, taking 49.5 percent of the popular vote and a majority of the electoral vote. A handful of votes were cast for the Liberty Party candidate, James G. Birney. It must have seemed to abolitionists like Phillips that the Free Soil Party did not seem to have much of a political future—not so long as the major national parties continued in their present state.[17]

Following the annexation of Texas in 1845, President Polk began preparations for a potential war with Mexico. The immediate issue was the border of the new republic—Texas claimed the Rio Grande, whereas Mexico insisted the boundary was the Nueces River, farther north. After a series of clashes along the border, Polk convinced Congress to declare war against Mexico. Though most Democrats and Whigs initially supported the war, John Quincy Adams and some other antislavery Whigs attacked the war as a Slave Power plot designed to expand slavery across North America. Meanwhile, the former Democratic congressman John P. Hale of New Hampshire had defied party leaders by denouncing the annexation of Texas, causing him to lose reelection in 1845. Hale joined with antislavery Whigs and the Liberty Party to found a new party in New Hampshire, the Free Soil Party and ran as its candidate. The New Hampshire legislature named him to the Senate in early 1847.[18]

Meanwhile, in August 1846, Polk asked Congress to appropriate $2 million in hopes of using that money as a down payment for the purchase of Alta California in another treaty with Mexico. During the debate over the appropriations bill, the Democratic congressman David Wilmot of Pennsylvania offered an amendment thereafter known as the Wilmot Proviso, which would ban slavery in any lands newly acquired from Mexico. Though broadly supportive of the war, Wilmot and some other antislavery northern Democrats regarded Polk, himself a proslavery southerner, as too favorable to southern interests in the party. Unlike some northern Whigs, Wilmot and other antislavery Democrats were largely unconcerned with the issue of racial equality, and instead opposed the expansion of slavery because they believed the institution was detrimental to the "laboring white man." The Wilmot Proviso passed the House with the support of both northern Whigs and northern Democrats, breaking the normal sectional pattern of partisan division in congressional votes, but it was defeated in the Senate. In February 1848, after the Mexican War, Mexican and American negotiators formulated the Treaty of Guadalupe Hidalgo, which provided for the cession of Alta California and New Mexico. Though many senators had reservations about the treaty, the Senate approved it in a 38–14 vote in February 1848. The New Mexico Territory, including parts of the future Colorado and Arizona, was added to the national domain, as was California, which had already revolted from Mexico and formed an independent republic (with help from US forces). With the Wilmot Proviso dead, the fate of slavery in these territories was uncertain.[19]

· · ·

With the debate over the annexation of Texas singeing national politics, the antislavery activist Lysander Spooner brought together and published arguments that the federal Constitution was an antislavery document. Spooner's New England ancestry was as ancient as Phillips's but hardly as illustrious. Spooner did not attend college but read law with leading Massachusetts lawyers and politicians, including the governor and later US senator John Davis, a Conscience Whig. Davis was a successful lawyer; his style of argument, based on close reading and logical perspective, made an impression on his student. State law until 1836 required noncollege men like Spooner to spend five years reading law, as opposed to three for college graduates. (Graduates of law schools had only to pass the bar exam.) Defying the licensing laws as examples of statist elitism, Spooner set up a practice in Worcester, Massachusetts, then largely a farming and small-business community on the Connecticut River. He argued that "no one has yet ever dared advocate, in direct terms, so monstrous a principle as that the rich ought to be protected by law from the competition of the poor."[20]

Spooner's book *The Unconstitutionality of Slavery*, released in 1845 in part as an extended answer to Phillips's collection, confronted Phillips's argument for free-state secession. Its 156 pages mixed natural law, custom, history, and statute to show that slavery was not only immoral but unconstitutional. After all, if law was merely the "requirement of natural justice," and if "no rule of civil conduct" could violate this basic principle, how could one man hold another in bondage? Even if there were exceptions to this basic principle, the Declaration of Independence (which Spooner regarded as fundamental law) reaffirmed it, as did the Articles of Confederation. The federal Constitution did not mention slavery, and Spooner believed that the absence of the term meant that slavery was a "mere abuse" imposed by force in some parts of the land. After all, the Constitution spoke of the "people" of the United States, and the persons within it. Hence it should be read as an antislavery document. If under it, both Congress and federal judges were obliged to undo the Slave Power and slave law, then abolitionists were compelled to work within the existing legal system. Spooner conceded that even if some among the framers wanted the federal government to protect slavery, the Constitution itself did not. Abolitionists such as Gerritt Smith of New York and Frederick Douglass cited Spooner approvingly in their work. The book was adopted by the founders of the Free Soil Party. Phillips decided that he had to challenge Spooner.[21]

Two years after Spooner published, Phillips opened his 108-page refutation of Spooner with the admission that had Spooner (and by proxy the

Liberty Party crew, including Alvan Stewart) proved his case, he and the whole abolition movement would have joined in praise of Spooner's presentation. Surely the abolitionists wanted Spooner to be right. "If beautiful theories could . . . oust from its place the ugly reality of a pro-slavery administration [of Polk]," he would "sit quiet" and let Spooner convert the nation. But he was not convinced.[22]

Phillips's refutation was a consequentialist one: that is, all he had to do was to show the ineffectuality of Spooner's case—that it had no impact on national politics, the federal courts, or the law. That was like shooting fish in a barrel. After all, the Free Soil Party did not change the results of the election of 1846. Nor was the Wilmot Proviso voted up in the Senate. Slavery still had many friends outside the South. But Phillips went beyond simple political facts to a more legalistic stance. Spooner was wrong about the Constitution. His "forced interpretation of legal maxims" was an exercise in futility. It led to a belief that the political system could be made into an antislavery engine. Such tomfoolery must be quashed. The crisis of slavery must be faced as a constitutional crisis; the Constitution, the courts, and Congress all seemed to agree that Spooner's position was wrong as a matter of law.[23]

For Phillips, the illogic of Spooner's wishful thinking was obvious. How could anyone believe that the courts, the Congress and the presidency were so warped that they supported the institution of slavery when the Constitution did not provide for it? Perhaps the politicians thought slavery a good thing. Southern leaders did. They agreed that slavery was good for the enslavers; it was good for the enslaved; it was good for the national economy. But if slavery was a patent wrong, then what could one conclude about the moral faculties of members of Congress, federal judges, and chief executives who were not Southerners? That answer would come in the "fiery trial" of a later time. For the present, Phillips insisted, "we ought to give up the experiment" of the federal Constitution and leave the Union.[24]

Spooner also argued that the officers of government must obey the law. If that law abetted slavery, then what was left for him? He was caught between the whimsy of his argument and the harsh facts. Only disobedience of the law could save the nation and free the enslaved. Thus the Constitution must be amended. Only then would the enslaved be safe. Until then, or at least until that prospect became real, an abolitionist could agree to live under the Constitution. So Phillips was right, and Spooner was wrong—conditions must be right for an amendment to the Constitution for abolitionists to live under it.

Phillips treated Spooner seriously, however, and not just because important abolitionists adopted Spooner's views. The space that Phillips devoted to Spooner's first chapter, "What is Law?" was a clue to Phillips's own view of law—and to how important law remained to him despite his abandonment of his law practice. Spooner, according to Phillips, simply passed by the issue of what law is, but Phillips, more of a trained legal counsel than Spooner, did not. For "all we have to do with law, is to find out what it practically is, and then amend it if we can." Spooner's view of law, according to Phillips, was a philosophical abstract—hardly the view a practicing lawyer would take, even though Spooner was still a member of the state bar. Phillips, no longer an active member, approached the law in a much more conventional manner: "Our only object is to abolish slavery, not to correct the fundamental ideas which men hold as to government." So he proposed to "dwell awhile" on Spooner's first chapter.[25]

Here Phillips demonstrated that the lawyer lurked behind the orator. In the space of a single reference note, he revealed that his three years of study at Harvard Law School were not lost. He kept his law books. He asked Spooner why he did not simply use Blackstone's definition of municipal or civil law instead of Spooner's own preferred natural law. Then he answered his own question. Blackstone defined law as "a rule of civil conduct, prescribed by a supreme power in a state, commanding what is right, and prohibiting what is wrong." This was John Austin's idea of legal positivism. (Spooner had not cited Austin.) A law might be just or unjust, but it must be obeyed. But Phillips's miniature lecture did not stop here. He then cited Austin in opposition to Blackstone: get rid of the right and wrong; law was simply the command of the state. Then he cited Chief Justice John Marshall and New York Chancellor James Kent to show that American jurisprudence accepted only the first part of Blackstone's rule. It was a marvelous (if slightly pedantic) display of formal legal doctrine. And it demonstrated that Phillips could summon legal argumentation and legal authority when he wanted to do so.[26]

Phillips's citation of Austin does pose two small mysteries. First, Austin himself credited Jeremy Bentham with originating the idea that law was simply the command of the state. Bentham was far better known than Austin when Austin, and later, Phillips wrote. Why not cite Bentham? One provocative answer is that Austin, unlike Bentham, found the authority of the state to be unitary and irresistible. For Phillips, this would be a far stronger version of his case that the federal government's sponsorship of slavery was compelling. I have no idea why Phillips did not cite Bentham, however. Second mystery: Story did not lecture on Austin when Phillips took courses at Harvard Law School. Story did not mention Austin once in any of the *Commentaries* on the law that Story was compiling from his lecture notes at the time. Phillips no doubt acquired a small law book library and kept it in his Boston office or at home, but there is no mention of Austin in Phillips's commonplace book or in any of his many speeches, or in his annotated work *The Constitution, A Pro Slavery Compact* of 1844. Nor had Spooner mentioned Austin. Phillips could of course have visited the Harvard Law School library and found there a copy of Austin, but however he found Austin, the point is that he knew what he was looking for and how to find it.[27]

Turning back to Spooner, who insisted that law was that which was morally right, Phillips asked what was to be done with law that was morally wrong. Following Spooner's logic, it was not law and therefore did not require obedience. One did not have to obey—indeed, one was obliged to disobey "a wicked constitution." Phillips agreed with Spooner that a judge holding office under such a constitution should decide cases under natural justice, not by wicked statutes and precedent. He did not learn this at Harvard Law School. In *Prigg v. Pennsylvania* (1842), Story had reluctantly ruled that the Constitution, statute, and precedent protecting slavery must be obeyed. So where was Phillips's disagreement with Spooner? Phillips thought that judges should resign rather than void laws or ignore them. In short, he was a legalist, whereas Spooner was an anarchist. To repeat, Phillips thought that the only legal action judges could take when faced with evil law was to take no part in its administration. This was the exact opposite of Story's position, and that of later judicial commentators such as the Yale Law School professor Robert Cover—that judges had to follow the law even if they found it morally repugnant.[28]

Phillips next offered that American government was based on contract, quoting Chief Justice John Jay and John Quincy Adams to prove the point. In other words, it was established that "the people and the office-holder make a contract" that the officeholder had to fulfill. If that contract is immoral, Spooner said, the people do not have to obey it. But if that contract is immoral, Phillips replied, then the government no longer exists. And that was where, Phillips concluded, Spooner was going. If judges were free to ignore statutes, then what was law in Maine might not be law in Mississippi. What was law today might not be law tomorrow. Hence, Spooner's jurisprudence was at war with itself. Here again, Phillips displayed his legal learning, and the legal method of briefing a case, to refute Spooner. What had started as a review of a book had become a plea in the court of public opinion in the cause of radical abolition versus natural-law anarchy. Phillips's essay was a legal brief, countering Spooner point by point, as conventional legal argument required. What no doubt seemed to readers then, and to historians later, a tiresome tirade, was anything but.[29]

There was an exception to Phillips's dire logic. Sitting in equity, might not a judge decide cases according to conscience? Was this a support for Spooner? Phillips railed against equitable discretion in a judge, calling it tyranny. He cited older English legal objections to unbridled discretion, then returned to Story. Story wrote an entire commentary on equity practice, the purpose of which was to lay down rules for judges sitting in equity and to expose students to the field. Phillips had apparently taken careful notes in class or hunted down a copy of Story's commentary when he prepared the review of Spooner. Showing off a little, he included the reference "see Story, *Equity*, volume 1, page 12." Thus he could (or thought he could) state, with authority, that the almost unanimous "voice of lawyers and judicial tribunals" agreed with him that judges were bound to follow the law as written. On this he added long quotations from William Blackstone, Justice James Iredell in federal district court, and Chief Justice John Marshall to make his point. (Obviously Phillips had copies of the *United States Reports* at hand; every law student had the four volumes of Blackstone's *Commentaries*.) Once again, the Harvard Law School graduate proved he could demolish the legal argument of a self-taught counselor. It also was a refutation of prevailing natural law jurisprudence in favor of legal positivism. But above all, it pulled the props out from under the Free-Soilers' constitutionalism.[30]

Spooner turned from judging in general to the federal Constitution as interpreted by the US Supreme Court. Phillips followed, reminding his readers that Spooner was discussing legal maxims, "arguing a law question, as such, on strictly *legal* principles, referring to legal authorities and rule" to support his argument (italics in original). Phillips treated the reader to a thorough interpretation of the Constitution on slavery, based on the Supreme Court's precedents. At the outset, Phillips conceded that where a decision of the Court was unclear, one might infer its meaning from the intentions of the justices. In other words, Phillips proposed to engage in plain text/original intent jurisprudence. In it, the commentator must rely on the sense in which words and ideas were used at the time by contemporaries. As authority for this mode of interpretation, Phillips cited Story's *Commentaries on the Constitution,* as well as a host of other legal authorities. He then followed John Marshall, James Kent, and Joseph Story to look for meaning in the language of the framers. And wherever one looked in the constitutional commentary of the founding era, according to Phillips, one found that the law of slavery was accepted. Did "the people" not know this? Were they ignorant of what they saw around them every day? That was impossible to believe, a "daring flight of genius" but a fiction.[31]

Phillips tracked Spooner through the clauses of the Constitution, state laws, and the decisions of the Supreme Court; through colonial history and the territories that became the national domain; through "Somerset's Case" (1772), in which Chief Justice Lord Mansfield found that slavery had no place in English law; and through Massachusetts Chief Justice Lemuel Shaw's opinion in *Commonwealth v. Aves* (1836) that even a temporary stay on free soil was enough to free enslaved persons brought to the state. Shaw worked through painstaking definitions of words such as *slavery* itself, with only one stumble over the Declaration of Independence. He recovered his footing by arguing that the Declaration was never binding on the states, nor on the United States, over and over making the case for the constitutionality of slavery more thoroughly than any of slavery's own advocates.[32]

And there was the irony. Phillips regarded Spooner as an ally, not an enemy, and did not denigrate him as he denigrated others who abetted the slave catchers and the proslavery judges. Yet if one did not know Phillips's own views, one might mistake him for a proslavery writer—that is, until the end (and the purpose) of the review. Phillips made clear that there could be no compromise with a law itself so compromised over slavery. Legally speaking, there was no way to deny the legality of slavery where domestic law and federal statute enabled it. So—as a lawyer and a legalist—Phillips had to conclude that Spooner was wrong. And it followed that no one who genuinely opposed slavery could remain in a Union that condoned it.

But why such a detailed refutation? Spooner's work was not that important in itself; it certainly was not because Spooner himself was a major figure. True, *The Unconstitutionality of Slavery* was Spooner's greatest work and his major contribution to the debate over slavery, but in itself it was not compelling, nor did it have much popularity except among other utopian abolitionists. Did Phillips, who decried gradualism, worry that some gradualist antislavery people, already attracted to the Free Soil Party, might be swayed away from immediatism by Spooner's essay? He did note that "we are told that the book, hoisted into undue notice by loud vaults of unthinking friends, was misleading wise men." Such mistakes had earlier led to the failure of the Liberty Party, which Free-Soilers such as Charles Sumner and the other Conscience Whigs seemed to have missed. Phillips had not, however, and warned that accepting political office in a proslavery government was a dead end for antislavery advocates. Was he waiting to see what happened to the Wilmot Proviso? Perhaps that was why Phillips had waited two years, from 1845, when Spooner published, to 1847, to reply to his essay.[33]

The response to the Wilmot Proviso did indeed prompt Phillips's reply, for he would later write that in the gap between 1845 and 1847, "how vigilantly, how patiently did we watch the Texas plot from its commencement! The politic South felt that its first move had been too bold, and thenceforward worked under-ground." It had seemed "impossible" to awaken antislavery to the Slave Power's plot. "I remember being one of a Committee which waited on [US Congressman] Abbott Lawrence, a year or two only before Annexation, to ask his countenance to some general movement, without distinction of party, against the Texas scheme. He smiled at our fears, begged us to have no apprehensions; stating that his correspondence with leading men at Washington enabled him to assure us Annexation was impossible, and that the South itself was determined to defeat the project. A short time after, Senators and Representatives from Texas took their seats in Congress!" But that was in 1845, so the timing of the delay was off.[34]

A different answer, one not tied to politics, elections, or parties, seems equally plausible. If one looks at the text of the review, at the marshalling of authorities and the detail of his argument, it seems that Phillips had taken the jurisprudential task seriously. One thinks of him as an orator and an agitator. One does not normally think of him as a legal treatise writer. But this was a man as well educated in the law as anyone in the country.

Phillips's immersion in an intellectual contest, motivated by taking Spooner seriously, would have been a welcome respite from the demands of abolitionism on the speaker's rostrum. One may be confused by the fact that so many of Phillips's speeches were published. But they were just that—published versions of what he had said as a speaker. Of course he prepared them for publication, but knowing that he did not write those orations out in advance, one recognizes that their written (published) versions were profoundly different from his review of Spooner—a two-year-long effort, filled with legal authorities, and nearly three times the length of his longest published speeches.

Spooner did not allow Phillips to have the last word. The contest between the Massachusetts and the New York abolitionists was by this time hot and heavy. In Part Second of his *Unconstitutionality of Slavery* (1847), a book of over 277 pages, Spooner made the argument that would be central to the Liberty Party and later to Abraham Lincoln's opposition to slavery. "The preamble expressly declares that 'We the people of the United States' establish the constitution for the purpose of securing justice, tranquility, defence, welfare, and liberty, to 'ourselves and our posterity.'" This language certainly implies that all "the people" who are parties to the Constitution, or join in establishing it, are to have the benefit of it, and of the laws made in pursuance of it. The only question, then, is, who were 'the people of the United States?'" His conclusion was equally prescient: "If these opinions are correct, it is the constitutional duty of Congress to establish courts, if need be, in every county and township even, where there are slaves to be liberated; to provide attorneys to bring the cases before the courts; and to keep a standing military force, if need be, to sustain the proceedings." When Phillips ignored Spooner's rejoinder, Spooner offered a third act: *A Defense for Fugitive Slaves* (1850). It was directed at the Fugitive Slave Acts of 1793 and 1850, rehearsing his earlier arguments that the Constitution was antislavery, so the acts of Congress must necessarily be unconstitutional on their face. At the very least, they relied entirely on ex parte evidence (the slave catcher's words alone), denied the putative fugitive a jury trial, required a summary judgment, and ignored the right to habeas corpus relief.[35]

· · ·

Intellectual tilting with Spooner (and by proxy with Spooner's allies) aside, it was Phillips's advocacy of disunionism that brought him into public disrepute even among some abolitionists. He had mentioned it as early as his lecture on the right of petition in 1837—before Garrison himself had promoted the idea. "Because time has shown that [slave law] sends out its poisonous branches over all our fair land, and corrupts the very air we breathe. Our fate is bound up with that of the South, so that they cannot be corrupt and we sound; they cannot fall, and we stand. Disunion is coming, unless we discuss this subject; for the spirit of freedom and the spirit of slavery are contending here for the mastery."[36]

Phillips further explored the idea of departing the Union in the early 1840s, not as an event, but as a program for the abolitionists who could not abide slavery in their midst. Still, it was not supported by the movement in general, but by the small coterie, the Boston Clique around Garrison, that met at Maria Weston Chapman's house a few blocks from Phillips's Exeter Street home. The men and women there reinforced each other's views and gave moral support to Phillips's own position. Maria Weston Chapman and Edmund Quincy, members of his own Brahmin caste, were closer to Phillips than was Garrison; Chapman was the "grand dame" of the clique. But Phillips was its penman, writing up and circulating most of the petitions and resolutions. With Quincy, he wrote the articles and pamphlets that kept the radical movement, and disunionism, in the public eye. As he wrote to Frederick Douglass in 1845, for the preface of the latter's *Narrative,* "the whole armory of northern law has no shield for [your freedom] . . . only those who trample the laws and the Constitution under their feet," thus ensuring that Douglass could safely publish his story and was free to speak in public.[37]

But why announce that abolitionists must advocate the end of the Constitution and the breakup of the Union? True, Garrison was now promoting the same notion, but Phillips was never a Garrison clone. Still, one answer in his own mind may have been that the Union and the Constitution were conceived in the sin of slavery. Abolitionists like Phillips abhorred sin, and making peace with slavery was the greatest sin of all. Was Phillips an idealist who did not see how unpopular his views of the Union and the Constitution would make him? Was he a perfectionist, of the sort increasingly common on the fringe of the reform frenzy of the antebellum North? Did his thinking parallel that of the Upstate New York Millerites of 1847, who waited for the end of days on the roofs of their houses? Or of the Oneida community members, who practiced free love? Or of the Shaker communities, who spurned the temptations of the flesh? Perhaps his aversion to the Constitution and the Union was merely a way to agitate his audiences, and in so doing, to be heard. It certainly gained him notoriety. Or perhaps it was a way of dissociating himself and the others in his circle from accommodationists such as William Henry Seward and the founders of the Liberty Party and the Free-Soilers. Some historians have found in his decision an attachment to an alternative, popular constitution, the constitution of the people out of doors. This version of antebellum constitutionalism is the centerpiece of certain modern theorists. But if this was one example of Americans manifesting "their constitutional commitments in the public sphere" rather than in courtrooms or legislative chambers, it was an odd way to do so. It would put him in the same camp as the anti-abolitionist rioters. In 1844, he even insisted that abolitionists must not vote, for voting would give credibility to the very same system that abetted slavery. In any case, along this road, he would find few fellow travelers.[38]

Even so, the road to reform in these years was filled with a variety of men and women whose ideas were even more extreme than Phillips's. Abby Kelley and her husband, Stephen Symonds Foster, shouted abolitionist line and verse from the pews of the established churches (from which they were unceremoniously tossed). Even Quakers and Baptists, whose origins in American religious life were contested, had no use for the Fosters' interruptions of their meetings. Parker Pillsbury, a rough-hewn New Hampshire abolitionist, was not so easily ushered out of churches. Thomas Wentworth Higginson, a Harvard graduate and former schoolteacher, went door to door signing up opponents of the Mexican-American War. Phillips knew them all, liked some more than others, but was aloof from their activities. They admired him. Higginson recalled that during the attempt to free the runaway Thomas Sims, Phillips was "strong throughout." But Phillips was discovering that his strong words were no more effective than their direct actions.[39]

CHAPTER 3

Radical

By the beginning of the 1850s, Phillips stood at the head of a group of radical reformers. In his personal habits and demeanor he was never an extremist, but his views had made him a target of both conservatives and liberals, in part because his place on the platform was almost guaranteed to bring jeers from some in the audience. The threat of personal attacks was real. But his foremost biographer finds that Phillips's oratory was having a sure, if limited, impact on the national discourse. He had estranged himself from many of his own Boston background, such as his fellow lawyer Benjamin Robbins Curtis; he had gained no friends among the moderates in either of the major political parties. This result ran parallel to party politics, itself becoming increasingly brittle and violent. Behind the turn to violence was the passage and implementation of the Fugitive Slave Act of 1850. For Phillips, organizing meetings, inviting major figures in intellectual life, keeping the abolitionist agenda alive, was never easy, but now more than ever seemed necessary.[1]

. . .

Although the fury of the Mexican-American War (1846–48) had ended, the furor over the Wilmot Proviso continued to roil national politics. One reason was that the former Mexican state of California, lately declaring itself an independent nation, was now ready to enter the United States. Its population had soared after the discovery of gold 100 miles from the eastern shore of the San Francisco Bay. On November 11, 1849, the voters ratified the draft California state constitution and sent it to Washington, DC. The document was long and detailed; indeed it took hours to transcribe the official copy, but it was clearly a free-state constitution. It began with a statement of rights, the first of which read, "All men are by nature free and independent, and have certain inalienable rights, among which are those of enjoying and defending life and liberty, acquiring, possessing, and protecting property: and pursuing and obtaining safety and happiness." It incorporated an expanded version of the federal Bill of Rights and spoke of persons or inhabitants of the state. Although the sections on political rights limited those persons to "white male" citizens, the law provided for joint property for wives, a reform based in part on Spanish/Roman law; made dueling illegal; and encouraged public education. Section 18 of Article I, however, was the most worrisome to southern members of the Senate and the Democratic leadership: "Neither slavery, nor involuntary servitude, unless for the punishment of crimes, shall ever be tolerated in this State." Section 3 of the same article seemed directed to the fugitive slave question: "The right of trial by jury shall be secured to all, and remain inviolate forever."[2]

In the Senate, southern opinion on the admission question grew sour and resentful. Leading southern Democrats condemned the admission of California as a violation of the Constitution (California had not been a territory) and a danger to the balance of power in the Senate (with the admission of California the free states would outnumber the slave states). Henry Clay, whose proposals had quieted congressional angst in the Missouri admission quarrel thirty years earlier, proposed a compromise— admit California and adopt a much more stringent Fugitive Slave Act, among other provisions.[3]

Under the Compromise of 1850, the new Fugitive Slave Act became law, and California was admitted to the Union. It provided for federal commissioners to assist in the rendition of alleged fugitives without their having benefit of due process (counsel, jury trial, confrontation and cross examination of witnesses). The act gave to the federal judiciary the power to name commissioners, and to require marshals to assist the commissioners:

> That when a person held to service or labor in any State or Territory of the United States, has heretofore or shall hereafter escape into another State or Territory of the United States, the person or persons to whom such service

or labor may be due, or his, her, or their agent or attorney, duly authorized, by power of attorney, in writing, acknowledged and certified under the seal of some legal officer or court of the State or Territory in which the same may be executed, may pursue and reclaim such fugitive person, either by procuring a warrant from some one of the [federal] courts, judges, or commissioners aforesaid, of the proper circuit, district, or county, for the apprehension of such fugitive from service or labor, or by seizing and arresting such fugitive, where the same can be done *without process*, and by taking, or causing such person to be taken, forthwith before such court, judge, or commissioner, whose duty it shall be to hear and determine the case of such claimant in a *summary manner.*

Lawyers in Massachusetts were soon choosing sides over the act. Whig leaders such as Daniel Webster defended the Compromise of 1850, including the Fugitive Slave Act, as necessary to save the Union. Not by chance, his major clients, Boston's textile and commercial interests, were closely aligned with southern cotton production. At the other end of the lists, antislavery men and abolitionists among the legal profession were determined that Boston would not become a handmaiden of the slave catchers. The enforcement of the Fugitive Slave Act of 1850 brought together a loose coalition of the anti-slavery lawyers—in some sense a section of the Massachusetts Bar. The leaders of this abolitionist section were all acquaintances of Phillips. Ellis Grey Loring, eight years Phillips's senior, preceded him at Harvard College and its infant law school. Loring represented suspected runaways and those who helped them to resist recapture. In other words, he sought remedies within the law. Sometimes he argued in court while antislavery protesters spirited runaways out of sight. Loring was one of the founders of the New England Anti-Slavery Society with Garrison and explained to the latter that slavery was legal but immoral, and its immorality had to be constrained by law. Loring died in 1858 at fifty, but others were already standing beside him in court next to bondsmen and -women. These included Richard Henry Dana Jr., another scion of old Puritanism who graduated from Harvard Law School and entered the bar in 1840. With Loring, he represented runaway' rescuers. So too did Boston's Samuel Edmund Sewall, a great-grandson of one of the first abolitionists. Like Loring and Dana, Sewall believed that the law allowed representation of suspected runaways, and argued for them in the Massachusetts courts. Charles Francis Adams, the son of John Quincy Adams, had urged passage of what became the 1843 Massachusetts Personal Liberty Law. It forbade state officials to participate in arrests of suspected runaways under the federal Fugitive Slave Act of 1793. All these men worked within the system. Phillips did not always agree with them, in particular with their views of race, but their legal activities paralleled his own arguments. Charles Sumner, after 1850 a senator from Massachusetts, carried their arguments to floor of the US Senate.[4]

More conservative antislavery lawyers also defended those who took the law into their own hands to free runaways from slave catchers. Antislavery politicians such as William Henry Seward believed that a regime of "relational" rights based on hospitality could eventually undo slavery. As governor of New York, he had refused to turn over to Virginia free Blacks who had abetted slave runaways. He later argued before the US Supreme Court the cause of John Van Zandt, who abetted the escape of a runaway; when fellow antislavery advocates were tried for attacking slave catchers, Seward donated funds to the resisters' defense. Above all these more conservative abolitionist lawyers wanted to prevent slavery from spreading throughout the nation. In the main, all of them were seen, and saw themselves, as righteous keepers of a higher law. Their goal was as simple as it was, at the time, unreachable: "to enlarge the canvass of law till it covers all men both black and white."[5]

After the 1850 law went into effect, Massachusetts antislavery bar members petitioned the state courts for injunctive relief against the rendition of alleged fugitives. The particular form of the writ was *de homine replegiando* (human replevin), a kind of pretrial habeas corpus. Chief Justice Lemuel Shaw showed no favor to these petitions; indeed, he considered them an affront to his dignity as well as to the dignity of his position. Phillips played only a minor part in this litigation, but when Benjamin Robbins Curtis stood in Faneuil Hall and defended both the act and Shaw, Phillips took fierce umbrage. Curtis was no friend of antislavery and had represented the enslaver in *Commonwealth v. Aves* in 1836, although later in his career, when he sat on the US Supreme Court, he would dissent in *Dred Scott v. Sandford* (1857).

． ． ．

The occasion for Phillips's philippic against Curtis was another visit by the British antislavery publicist George Thompson. When Thompson was driven from Boston by a mob, Phillips welcomed him to Lynn on November 26, 1850, and gave a talk in his honor. The agitation over the Fugitive Slave Act was reaching the boiling point. Curtis had thrown fuel on the fire by defending the act earlier in the year.

How would Phillips defeat Curtis's arguments in favor of the act? The answer was plain to Phillips. Just as he had in refuting Spooner, he must rely on his skill and learning as a lawyer. Again as in his exchange with Spooner, Phillips did not have a paying client. Or rather, his client was the people. This was Phillips as the public interest lawyer. The people would judge. Massachusetts had become a virtual courtroom. Phillips weighed in: "Mr. Curtis defended the right of Massachusetts to surrender the fugitive slave, on the ground that every sovereign State had authority to exclude foreigners from its soil." Whether a runaway was a foreigner or not, Curtis had to assume that the runaway was a person in the law, subject to it. But slave law in the United States regarded the enslaved as property, rather than persons. Phillips seized on this initial irony. 'Exclude foreigners from the soil'! How delicate a phrase! What a 'commodity of good names' this trouble of ours has coined!" For in name the slave was a commodity. Phillips's audience recognized the point.[6]

But had not the Constitution a Rendition Clause (Article IV, section 2, clause 3) clearly aimed at runaways? And had not Congress twice, in 1793 and 1850, explicitly provided the mechanism for enforcement of the clause? The Constitution never mentioned slavery or the enslaved. But what was in a name, or the absence of it? Spooner had made much of the absence of the word *slave*, but Phillips was not persuaded by Spooner's argument. In law, names had force. In oratory, names were no less potent and more vulnerable to parody. The framers knew that "service and labor" was the "Constitutional veil to hide the ugly face of slavery." The Slave Power hid its viciousness behind names. "Then, 'Peculiar institution'! 'Patriarchal institution'!! 'Domestic institution'!!! And now, 'excluding foreigners from our soil!!!!'"[7]

Phillips wondered, sarcastically, how a person of color whose ancestors for five generations had lived and toiled in the South could still be called (as they were by Curtis) a "foreigner"? The power of naming was an old one, as old as magic, as old as the first Europeans who took Indian lands by rechristening them with Spanish names. "But let us, meantime, be careful to use all plainness of speech—to call things rigorously by their right names." The agents of the runaways' enslavers were slave-catchers and nothing less. Phillips was adamant: do not mollify those who commit injustices. "Heed no cry of 'harsh language.' Yield not to any tenderness of nerves more sensitive than the conscience they cover."[8]

In plain language, Phillips laid out the legal argument against Curtis and his Whig allies and his reasons for condemning the 1850 Fugitive Slave Act. The act violated all customary and statutory norms of due process. It provided for commissioners, appointed by the circuit courts, who could take evidence and summarily order the return of suspected runaways. The state itself could not intervene. Nor did the suspect have the due process rights in the federal Constitution, to wit the right to counsel, to produce evidence, and to have a jury trial of the facts as outlined in the Fourth, Fifth, and Sixth Amendments. Thus slave catchers from the South could succeed with ex parte (one side only) evidence from the slave catcher's employer. The putative slaveholder need not appear or testify under oath that so and so was a fugitive in order to justify the capture, or themselves capture, any person and bring them before the commissioners.[9]

The problem was not just the overruling of the procedural guarantees in the Bill of Rights, which mentions persons—not citizens, let alone free persons—but the danger that such a summary process in the hands of unelected officials (the commissioners, like the judges, were not elected), posed to free persons of color. As Phillips put it, the statute's title should be changed to the "Bill for the more safe and speedy kidnaping of persons of color." As mentioned above, the evidence for the recaption (recapture) was ex parte—that is, it was not tested in court and came from one of the interested parties (the putative enslaver). The act gave to a private citizen (the slave catcher or the enslaver) the right to take the body of another person, and carry it to "who knows where" by an authority against which no one could object. The law was a "wide open gate for avarice and perjury" that no one could close. The idea that civil disputes gave both parties the chance to prove their case had disappeared in Congress's haste to assuage the anger of the South at the admission of California as a free state. That admission was democratic—that is, it was based on the vote of Californians. The Fugitive Slave Act was the very opposite, taking from Massachusetts courts and its people the right to determine their own laws, and the rights of their own citizens.[10]

"Recaption" under the Fugitive Slave Act was shorthand for "no due process." The only evidentiary requirement for the slave catchers was that their victim was Black. Some runaways did succeed in escaping before the slave catchers could secure their prey. Shadrach Minkins, a runaway, was carried to the courthouse by the sheriff. He was represented by Richard Henry Dana Jr.. Minkins was later rescued by two other free Blacks and surrounded by a crowd of cheering men, then whisked away to Cambridge and thence to freedom farther north. But the rescue was an anomaly, with an antislavery mob reversing the conduct of the antiabolitionist mobs of earlier years. Phillips had nothing to do with it, as he was busy escorting George Thompson to Springfield. In the pages of the *Liberator,* however, William Lloyd Garrison defended the mob for its "love of liberty," and Phillips agreed.[11]

But Phillips saw how pyrrhic victories like Minkins's were. President Millard Fillmore, aided by Secretary of State Daniel Webster, issued a proclamation condemning the rescue of Minkins, something no president or secretary of state had ever done in response to antiabolitionist violence. Fillmore declared he was "calling on all well-disposed Citizens, to rally to the support of the Laws of their Country, and requiring and commanding all officers, civil and military, and all other persons, civil or military, who shall be found within the vicinity of this outrage, to be aiding and assisting, by all means in their power, in quelling this, and other such combinations, and assisting the Marshal and his Deputies in recapturing the above mentioned prisoner; and I do, especially, direct, that prosecutions be commenced against all persons who shall have made themselves aiders or abettors in or to this flagitious offence." In future, this proclamation would array federal troops against any attempt to rescue slaves in Boston. Fillmore's unprecedented overreaction to the case was a victory for southern Democrats and "Cotton" Whigs, and, at the same time, a confirmation of Phillips's disunionism.[12]

·   ·   ·

Phillips revealed that he saw himself as a public interest lawyer in his essay "Public Opinion." The ostensible subject was again Benjamin Robbins Curtis's defense of the Fugitive Slave Act. But Phillips went beyond Curtis to a general discussion of racism and law, exploring the legal roots of "colophobia" [*sic*] in the nation. "We live under a government of men. The

Constitution is nothing in South Carolina, but the black law is everything. The law that says the colored man shall sit in the jury-box in the city of Boston is nothing. Why? Because the Mayor and Aldermen, and the Selectmen of Boston, for the last fifty years, have been such slaves of colophobia [*sic*], that they did not choose to execute this law of the Commonwealth. I might go through the statute-book, and show you the same result."[13]

The reference to the (state of Massachusetts) statute book reminded his audience that racial bias had extended its tentacles into every phase of lawmaking. Thus the law itself became the handmaiden of the slavocracy. "Mr. Curtis forgot to finish his argument, and show us how, *in present circumstances*, it is moral in us to *exercise this legal right*. I may have, by law, the right to exclude the world from my house; but surely there are circumstances, as in the case of a man dying on my threshold, where it would be gross inhumanity, utter sin before God, to exercise that right." Here Phillips echoed (borrowed?) from William Henry Seward's idea of relational rights. Hospitality, what every man owed to every other man on the threshold of their door, was an older law than the Constitution. "Surely, the slave's claim on us is equal. How exactly level to the world's worst idea of a Yankee, this pocket argument that the Commonwealth would suffer by yielding to its noblest instincts; that Massachusetts cannot now afford to be humane, to open her arms, a refuge, in the words of her own statute of 1642, for all who "*fly to her from the tyranny and oppression of their persecutors!*"[14]

Phillips's reasons to reject Curtis's argument rested on strong democracy. Curtis "did not touch, or even glance at, the *popular* objection to the Fugitive Slave Bill, which is not that fugitive slaves are to be given up according to its provisions, but that its right name is, 'A Bill for the more safe and speedy kidnapping of free colored people.'" If the law must be obeyed—a central tenet of positivism—that tenet, in turn, must rest on the will of the people. The "people" included people of color: "Every man found on Massachusetts soil has a right, until the contrary is shown, to be considered a free man, this bill [reducing the Fugitive Slave Act to its previous stage as a bill in Congress] recognizes the right, *not in the remotest manner alluded to in the Constitution*, of certain other persons to arrest and transport [a runaway] elsewhere, without judge, warrant, process, or reason rendered to anybody; and even in cases of resistance to this, allows such a man to be carried hence on *ex parte* evidence, of whose manufacture he had no notice, gotten up nobody knows where and by whom nobody has authority to inquire!"[15]

The result violated every common-law tenet of evidence and due process. "And that we are called to put implicit confidence in the peculiarly conscientious and striking reluctance of slaveholders to trespass on the rights of others, that this loose law, this wide-open gate for avarice and perjury, shall never be abused!" Finally, and most important, was the way that the Fugitive Slave Act violated the right to a jury trial. "And, further still, we are told not to be anxious about the checks and safeguards of jury trial. . . . The [alleged] *slave's* jury trial (not a matter of right, but granted when he finds some one willing to run the risk of paying single, perhaps double, costs, and in some States, only if the Court pleases, even then), subject to lashes if the suit be held groundless, the jury-box filled probably with slave-holders, a witness box closed against all men of his own race, and the burden of proof on him to show that the claimant does not own him according to Southern law!"[16]

By now Phillips had so often abjured any allegiance to the United States and any of its laws that were friendly to slavery that he was a pariah to all but the Garrisonians. He did not reject the laws or the constitution of the Commonwealth, however. In this, he was something of a states' rights theorist. He did not think out the implications of this stance, nor see how it mirrored that of the slave states. But so long as Massachusetts protected the runaway, Phillips remained loyal to it. Actually, his loyalty was to an idealized version of its history, purified in his telling. The Massachusetts of the first Puritan emigrants such as the colonial governor Henry Vane and the revolutionary Massachusetts of Samuel Adams—these were his guiding lights. His own family interest coincided with this history, for Phillips had never lost the passion for genealogy, in particular the genealogy of the Phillips family, that had absorbed his twenties. He linked his own principles and advocacy of liberty to that of his (imagined) ancestors and those in the Commonwealth's past who resembled them. In all his orations, he never failed to call on these avatars. But he was no antiquarian. The past was always the present for him, and at no time more than when he had to protest the rendition of runaway slaves.[17]

Throughout the 1850s, although he was never the attorney of record for any Blacks accused of being runaways, Phillips played a role in what one historian has called "resistance lawyering." In over 40 percent of the cases brought to commissioners under the Fugitive Slave Act, lawyers managed to short-circuit the summary provisions of the act. By demanding evidence, causing procedural delays, and even aiding and abetting escapes and purchases, the resistance lawyers managed to gain freedom for runaways. Operating in concert with local vigilance committees and antislavery protesters, they reversed the practice of the proslavery gangs of the 1830s. They mobbed officials and surrounded jails where suspected runaways were kept. Phillips was a leader of the Boston vigilance committee, and aided their efforts by signing petitions and giving testimony, and even helping runaways evade or resist recaption. Although other resistance lawyers did not cross this line—for example Richard Henry Dana and Richard Hildreth in Boston—Phillips not only did but urged others to do so.[18]

. . .

Although there was no necessary connection between abolitionism and feminism, there was both a logical connection and a personal one for Phillips. Because of his marriage, Phillips's closest support group was his wife and her friends, all elite Boston-area women. They were committed to antislavery, in part because of their general belief in the improvement of morals, and in part because antislavery was one of the few avenues in which educated and committed women could engage in public life. In law, married women were subordinate to their husbands, their property his to acquire, use, and sell. With a few exceptions, this *feme covert* regime extended into all areas of domestic relations law. It was a natural leap for such women to see their position in society as a kind of bondage; for them antislavery became a species of feminism.[19]

In some ways the feminist and the antislavery movements were parallel. In both, free white men spoke for the rights of others. But this was not always so. At the first women's rights convention at Seneca Falls, New York, in 1848, Elizabeth Cady Stanton sounded the trumpet for women's right to vote in a Declaration of Sentiments: "[Man] has never permitted her to exercise her inalienable right to the elective franchise. He has compelled her to submit to laws, in the formation of which she had no voice. He has withheld from her rights which are given to the most ignorant and degraded men—both natives and foreigners. Having deprived her of this first right of a citizen, the elective franchise, thereby leaving her without representation in the halls of legislation, he has oppressed her on all sides."[20]

Phillips was not only in sympathy with these ideas but also spoke in support of the women's Declaration. At a Worcester convention on October 15, 1851, he explained that "the right of suffrage for women is, in our opinion, the corner-stone of this enterprise, since we do not seek to protect woman, but rather to place her in a position to protect herself." He conceded that "no political community or nation ever existed in which women have not been in a state of political inferiority. But, in reply, we remind our opponents that the same fact has been alleged, with equal truth, in favor of slavery." The two causes were in his mind not only parallel but deeply intertwined: "We deny the right of any portion of the species to decide for another portion, or of any individual to decide for another individual, what is and what is not its proper sphere."[21]

The message and the resolution therein rested squarely on Phillips's legalism—his advocacy of a public interest cause and his faith in strong democratic positivism. Morality and sentiment to one side, "It is enough for our argument that natural and political justice, and the axioms of English and American liberty, alike determine that rights and burdens, taxation and representation, should be coextensive; hence women, as individual citizens, liable to punishment for acts which the laws call criminal, or to be taxed in their labor and property for the support of government, have a self-evident and indisputable right, identically the same right that men have, to a direct voice in the enactment of those laws and the formation of that government." Rights and burdens together mandated full legal quality. If "the time has been when it was the duty of the reformer to show cause why he appeared to disturb the quiet of the world," that cause was a universal one—for all those unjustly treated. Women's rights and antislavery went hand in hand.[22]

. . .

As 1851 ended, Phillips admitted that some of the energy of the attempted rescues had gone, and along with it, the prospects for further reform. On January 28, 1852, he told an antislavery meeting in Boston, "To some, it may seem that we had more sources of interest and of public excitement on that occasion than we have now. We had with us, during a portion, at least, of that session [George Thompson], the eloquent advocate of our cause on the other side of the water. We had the local excitement and the deep interest which the first horror of the Fugitive Slave Bill had aroused." Could words rouse the forces of antislavery, when events told against them? He hoped so. "Give us time. . . . Talk is all powerful. We are apt to feel ourselves overshadowed in the presence of colossal institutions. We are apt, in coming up to a meeting of this kind, to ask what a few hundred or a few thousand persons can do against the weight of government, the mountainous odds of majorities, the influence of the press, the power of the pulpit, the organization of parties, the omnipotence of wealth." But in the end, the abolitionists' voices would sway public opinion, if they did not lose faith in the movement: "Each man here, in fact, holds his property and his life dependent on the constant presence of an agitation like this of anti-slavery. Eternal vigilance is the price of liberty." Phillips was the ultimate democrat, an individualist with a highly developed (if somewhat brittle) conscience. This was the very opposite of the traditional authority figure: "A man gets up in the pulpit, or sits on the bench, and we allow ourselves to be bullied by the judge or the clergyman, when, if he stood side by side with us, on the brick pavement, as a simple individual, his ideas would not have disturbed our clear thoughts an hour. Now the duty of each anti-slavery man is simply this,—Stand on the pedestal of your own individual independence, summon these institutions about you, and judge them."[23]

The speech on public opinion marked a stage in the evolution of Phillips's own strong democratic positivism. It had not developed into organized political activity, along the lines that the Liberty Party and the Free-Soil Party advocated. It did not devolve into anarchy, as had Spooner's views. Instead, it straddled the problem of resistance to law. Phillips essayed an intellectual reformulation of abolition. For him, resistance to slave law was not resistance to law at all, but a call for a democratic referendum on law, placing it in the people's hands. He had become the spokesman of a strong democracy, in which all the people play some part in self-governance.[24]

But the calm reflection of "Public Opinion" was matched by Phillips's passion for radical change in these days. One sees the smoldering frustration in "The Surrender of Sims," read to the Massachusetts Anti-Slavery Society on January 30, 1852. This was an essay on the incapacity of the liberal legal process, of playing the game of antislavery from within the existing legal system. Recall that the previous April, city officials had marshalled over a hundred armed police officers, abetted by a similar number of proslavery volunteers, to convey twenty-three-year-old Thomas Sims to Boston harbor, and thence back to slavery. This violent end to Sims's case was chilling evidence of the compliance of state officialdom with slave law. Phillips roared that the highest court of the Commonwealth (he meant Chief Justice Shaw) had abetted the surrender of Sims. "I was once a member of the profession myself. But glad I am so no longer, since the head of it has bowed his burly person [a poke at Shaw's girth] to Francis Tukey's chain [a reference to the actual chain that the town marshal had placed around the jailhouse to prevent the rescue of Sims]." Shaw, who had earlier in *Aves*, the "Slave Med" case (1836), found a reason not to return Med, an enslaved girl brought to Massachusetts by a slaveholder, had now betrayed the bench and the courts of the Commonwealth and the "honor of a noble profession" by allowing the removal of Sims.[25]

In this lecture, delivered on the first anniversary of the rendition of Sims, Phillips explained why the Fugitive Slave Act violated due process. The essence of abiding by the law is that the law officer obeys the law. In case after case, as in Sims's, "Many of these cases have been a perversion, not only of all justice, but of all law. . . . The merciful and safe rule has always been, that an officer, arresting any one wrongfully, shall not be permitted to avail himself of his illegal act for the service of a true warrant while he has the man in custody. This would be not only a sanction, but an encouragement, of illegal detention. But, in several of these cases, the man has been seized on some false pretense, known to be a sham, and then the authorities allowed those having him in custody to waive the prosecution of the pretended claim, and serve upon him the real warrant." Phillips saw a violation of the basic principles of law not only permitted but encouraged by the Fugitive Slave Act.[26]

Had Phillips finally lost all faith in the law? The answer is no. This address reaffirmed that the law, rightly understood, should have maintained Sims's freedom. "While judges and executives deserted their posts, the abolitionists violated no law. They begged for nothing but the law,— they wearied themselves to obtain the simple legal rights guaranteed to them and to all by the State. The city government, in direct defiance of [John Quincy Adams Jr.'s Personal Liberty Law] of 1843, aided, both directly and indirectly, in the arrest and detention of a person claimed as a slave." Was this merely higher law? No, it was rooted in a state statute and in precedent. Phillips was being lawyerly.[27]

Obviously, abolitionist agitation had failed to move the nation; it had even failed to convince Massachusetts antislavery advocates to help free Sims. Although the Free Soil Party's growth in numbers hinted that slavery would not be able to expand into free territory, this was not what the abolitionists would call a victory, for it did not touch slavery where it existed.

On that question, Phillips did not urge violence. He urged patience instead, trusting that public opinion would in the end win out against slavery. But his patience was wearing thin.[28]

. . .

As the woeful effects of the Fugitive Slave Law in Massachusetts were becoming all too plain to see, Phillips's review of the abolitionist movement in midcourse—"The Philosophy of the Abolitionist Movement"—clung to the doctrine of strong democratic positivism. Phillips was not just explaining his own commitment or the ideas of the movement but giving a resonant voice to what he believed to be the highest ideals and aspirations of the nation. Thus, on January 27, 1853, he told the Massachusetts Anti-Slavery Society meeting that so long as the abolitionists would not quit the field, these ideals would remain vibrant, whatever the Slave Power did with the nation's politics. He conceded, "I wish . . . to notice some objections that have been made to our course." Then he brilliantly segued into showing that abolitionism was Americanism at its best. Phillips not only spoke for and to abolitionists. He spoke for and to the enslaved: "For the slave's sake, we reiterate our explanations, that he may lose no tittle of help by the mistakes or misconceptions of his friends." Alongside the contemporary, moralistic, and political comments, the "Christian Love," and the "Christian frankness," lay a powerful legalist thesis.[29]

A telling point for his case was the comparison with Britain and British law. Reformers there had used the legal apparatus to end slavery. Those who belittled that achievement were wrongheaded. "If the men who, by popular agitation, outside of Parliament, wrung from a powerful oligarchy Parliamentary Reform, and the Abolition of the Test Acts, of High Post Rates, of Catholic Disability, of Negro Slavery and the Corn Laws, did 'not win anything,' it would be hard to say what winning is." The comparison with the American antislavery movement was patent: "I claim for the Anti-Slavery movement with which this Society is identified, that, looking back over its whole course, and considering the men connected with it in the mass, it has been marked by sound judgment, unerring foresight, the most sagacious adaptation of means to ends, the strictest self-discipline, the most thorough research, and an amount of patient and manly argument addressed to the conscience and intellect of the nation." All of this did not sound like, and was not, the bombast of an agitator but the preparation for a great national legal case, exactly how counsel would prepare briefs and oral argument, and then name the remedy. The model was not the constrained common-law writ pleading, however, in which the remedy was monetary, but an equitable remedy, a grand injunction, forbidding slavery itself.[30]

In what court might the counsel of the abolitionists then win the day? The stakes were high, the dangers all around. For the public interest lawyer who believed in strong democracy, the answer was plain: public opinion. "We are fighting a momentous battle at desperate odds—one against a thousand. Every weapon that ability or ignorance, wit, wealth, prejudice or fashion can command, is pointed against us." The metaphor of a legal contest as a battle was so worn down that it was almost a cliché. But litigation in American courts was adversarial. Among the best litigators were those whose oratorical powers were as able, or even abler, than their research in the law. What was more, outside every hall where the antislavery band met, an armed mob might be waiting. It had happened already more than once. But "our clients are three millions of Christian slaves, standing dumb suppliants at the threshold of the Christian world. They have no voice but ours to utter their complaints, or to demand justice."[31]

Though he might never step into a courtroom again (save when he gave his evening lectures), Phillips cast himself in the role of the movement's legal counsel, and the enslaved as its virtual clients. And what was the indictment? "It is simply holding the intelligent and deliberate actor responsible for the character and consequences of his acts." This was the very core of criminal justice—that the voluntary commission of a criminal act by a person or persons capable of seeing wrong was culpable. "This we may claim—we have never judged a man but out of his own mouth. We have seldom, if ever, held him to account, except for acts of which he and his own friends were proud." Phillips's habits of mind, honed by law school and practice, even brief practice, remained in place.[32]

What precisely was the crime? It was not just the imposition of labor without payment, or the denial of basic rights such as freedom of speech, of movement, and of domestic identity. After all, chattel slavery was legal. But rape was not—even under existing slave law. Thus he framed the indictment: "The South is one great brothel, where half a million of women are flogged to prostitution, or, worse still, are degraded to believe it honorable." That the enslaved were the victims of these crimes could not be doubted— but it was not only doubted, it was denied. On top of this, agents of the slavocracy committed a second criminal offense: "Free men are kidnapped in our streets, to be plunged into that hell of slavery, and now and then one, as if by miracle, after long years, returns to make men aghast with his tale." Why, then, did so many in the free North refuse to accuse the slave South of the crime? It was because in the North, slavemongering had allies.[33]

Who argued the case *for* slavery in the public arena? The answer was plain—it was the critics of the antislavery movement. They accused Phillips and his cohort of impatience, of uncharitable language, of rabble rousing. They led the southern wing of the Democratic Party and the Cotton Whigs. They reached into the financial capitals of the North and the textile mills of New England. Thus Phillips had not only to make the case against slavery and the enslavers but he also had to defend his own conduct. Had the case been made in the marketplace, he would have spoken of dollars and sense. Had it been in a college, he would have spoken as a scholar. Were it in a church, he would have sermonized. But his courtroom was public opinion, a public opinion that had been radicalized by the opposition to abolition. That was (and is) a kind of incivility that even the most avid representation in court avoids. One does not impugn the motives or methods of one's opposing counsel—unless, of course, one does. "Our object is not to make every man a Christian or a philosopher, but to induce every one to aid in the abolition of slavery. We expect to accomplish our object long before the nation is made over into saints, or elevated into philosophers." And that is why contemporary and later scholarly observers of Phillips missed the underlying legalism of his agitation.[34]

What was left? With education, religion, politics, and philosophy unable to defeat the Slave Power, what could win the slaves their freedom? Information. "From this band of men has proceeded every important argument or idea that has been broached on the Anti-Slavery question from 1830 to the present time." Even the Free Soil movement and its political leaders had not come to the necessary conclusion. Political bargaining and campaigning would not work, for the slave interest was too well entrenched in the national government. "Before that jury we summon you. We are weak here—out-talked, out-voted." There was only one answer—one legal answer—that would protect freedom against slavery: leave the Union.[35]

Whom did Phillips choose to follow, and what was the path? "I will begin with certainly the ablest and perhaps the most honest statesman who has ever touched the slave question. Any one who will examine John Quincy Adams's speech on Texas, in 1838, will see that he was only seconding the full and able exposure of the Texas plot." Adams was a lawyer; his twin aims were antislavery and freedom of speech. The "Texas plot" was an attempt by the Slave Power to bring Texas, newly independent from Mexico, into the Union as four separate states. The battle was a political one but fought with votes in Congress. Phillips's focus on Adams led next to the gag rule battle. "Look next at the Right of Petition. Long before any member of Congress had opened his mouth in its defence, the Abolition presses and lecturers had examined and defended the limits of this right, with profound historical research and eminent constitutional ability." All the agitation—the meetings, the publications, the speeches— had legal aims. "Lawyers and statesmen have tacitly settled down into its full acknowledgment." In response to the feeble efforts of the Coloni- zation Society, "Judge [William] Jay followed with a work full and able, establishing every charge by the most patient investigation of facts."[36]

What had been the result? Alas, not progress. "On the constitutional questions which have at various times arisen,—the citizenship of the col- ored man, the soundness of the *Prigg* decision, the constitutionality of the old Fugitive Slave Law, the true construction of the slave-surrender clause,—nothing has been added, either in the way of fact or argument, to the works of Jay, Weld, Alvan Stewart, E. G. Loring, S. E. Sewall, Rich- ard Hildreth, W. I. Bowditch, the masterly Essays of the *Emancipator* at New York, and the *Liberator* at Boston, and the various addresses of the Massachusetts and American Societies for the last twenty years."[37]

But what of the Free Soil movement? Had that not stopped the move- ment of the Slave Power into the territories? Phillips had already ex- plained why Lysander Spooner and the Free Soil Party were intellectu- ally and politically bankrupt. By arguing that the Constitution was not proslavery, they had conceded the practical point to the slave interest by allowing slavery to exist. They thought that a political solution was suffi- cient. It had not proven so. "If it has either merit or truth, they are due to no legal learning recently added to our ranks, but to some of the old and well-known pioneers. This claim has since received the fullest investiga- tion from Mr. Lysander Spooner, who has urged it with all his unrivalled ingenuity, laborious research, and close logic. He writes as a lawyer, and has no wish, I believe, to be ranked with any class of anti-slavery men." That was unfair. We have seen that Spooner was antislavery, but Phillips saw the world in black and white.[38]

Phillips's public speaking targeted the judges and commissioners who aided the slave catchers, even when the officials simply enforced the Fugitive Slave Act. Thus, when counsel for the runaway Thomas Sims sought Chief Justice Lemuel Shaw's aid in delaying the hearing on Sims's rendition in 1851, the chief justice not only refused but found that the Necessary and Proper Clause and the Rendition Clause made the Fugitive Slave Act of the preceding year constitutional. Now federal authority was added to the scales against the runaways and the abolitionists. Shaw's views were clear and fixed on the basis of well-settled practice and principle. But the principle was a legal one—the writ would not be returned and the prisoner's case heard because it could not, in his mind, prevail.[39]

. . .

More evidence of the illicit union of free state officials and slave state interests arrived the next year, in the Anthony Burns affair. As a port city whose trade included coastal shipping from and to the South, Boston was a natural haven for slaves hiding on ships leaving southern ports. Anthony Burns's case again brought the Boston Vigilance Committee from the lecture hall into the streets. The trial of Burns, a fugitive slave from Virginia, occurred in Boston before commissioner Edward Greely Loring during the spring of 1854. Working as a hired hand in Richmond, Burns had saved money and stowed away on a ship to Boston, where he worked in a clothing store. A letter home to his brother unintentionally revealed his location, and when it was intercepted, Burns's slaveholder, Charles F. Suttle, traveled north and claimed Burns under the Fugitive Slave Act of 1850. Members of the vigilance committee attempted to free Burns from custody. The rescue effort was unsuccessful, and a guard was killed in the process. At the trial, Burns's lawyers argued that the Fugitive Slave Act was unconstitutional and that Burns was not actually the man whom Suttle claimed to own. On June 1, 1854, Commissioner Loring, a Whig associated with Webster's part of the party and an opponent of free soil, ruled against Burns, who was afterward transported to Norfolk, Virginia, on a US revenue cutter. Antislavery activists later purchased his freedom, and he became a minister, dying in Canada in 1862. None of those responsible for the guard's death was convicted. Many southerners believed that, in spite of the Fugitive Slave Act's successful enforcement, the Burns affair proved that northerners could not be trusted to fulfill their constitutional obligations.[40]

Phillips had joined with other antislavery orators at Faneuil Hall to argue for Burns's freedom and turned his wrath on Loring. After Burns had been returned to Virginia, Phillips presented petitions urging the legislature and the governor to throw Loring out of his post as judge of probate, a much more lucrative position than federal commissioner, and one that the governor controlled. "[We] ask you to remove a Judge of Probate, who has shown that he is neither a humane man nor a good lawyer. In the whole of my remarks, Gentlemen, I beg you to bear in mind that we, the petitioners, are asking you to remove, not a judge merely, but a Judge of Probate. A magistrate who is, in a peculiar sense, the counsellor of the widow and the fatherless. The family, in the moment of terrible bereavement and distress, must first stand before him. To his discretion and knowledge are committed most delicate questions, large amounts of property, and very dear and vastly important family relations." The petition then explained that removing Loring would not undermine the independence of the bench but strengthen it. "You have given no higher title than that of a Massachusetts Judge to Sewall, to Sedgwick, to Parsons. Take it away, then, from one who volunteers, hastens, to execute a statute which the law as well as the humanity of the nineteenth century regards as infamous and an outrage. We come before you, not to attack the Bench, but to strengthen it, by securing it the only support it can have under a government like ours,- the confidence of the people." Phillips's appeal to strong democratic positivism was here folded into the public interest in removing Loring from office.[41]

Once again in a legal setting, Phillips reverted to the habits and language of the law. These were never far from him, even in the pitched battles against the Fugitive Slave Act and its servants. So when he needed authority, he turned to the report of the committee on the judiciary, composed of the leading bench and bar, that had advised the state constitutional convention in 1820: "Remember, Gentlemen, that I read the following extracts, not to show the opinion of this Convention as to the value or the danger of this power; I merely wish to show you that, in the opinion of the ablest lawyers of the State, the Constitution, as it then stood, (and it stands now precisely as it stood then,) gave to this Legislature unlimited authority to remove judges, for any cause they saw fit; and that, while all the speakers were fully aware of its liability to abuse, no speaker denied its unlimited extent, or proposed to strike the power from the Constitution." To his side he summoned Lemuel Shaw, Daniel Webster, and others who urged obedience to law and order (and the Fugitive Slave Act). Lawyers routinely quoted from those with whom, on other occasions, they had disputed. The habits of lawyering did not die hard; they did not die at all in Phillips's thinking. They could be—and were—summoned when appropriate.[42]

Like John Quincy Adams, Phillips understood that the suppression of the abolitionist movement was simultaneously a suppression of free speech. An anti-abolitionist mob was aided by government officials in imposing this unconstitutional practice. In 1855, recalling the Boston mob that drove George Thompson from the town and William Lloyd Garrison from the speaker's platform, Phillips thanked his allies: "Never open the statute-book of Massachusetts without thanking Ellis Gray Loring and Samuel J. May, Charles Follen and Samuel E. Sewall, and those around me who stood with them, for preventing [Governor] Edward Everett from blackening it with a law making free speech an indictable offense."[43]

. . .

In 1857, as President James Buchanan's administration took office, and the cabinet was filled witih proslavery Democrats, Phillips's hopes for reform faded. John C. Frémont, the Republican candidate, had won electoral votes in the North, but he did not seem radical enough to Phillips. Buchanan asked US Supreme Court Chief Justice Roger B. Taney to end the raging dispute over slavery in the territories. In a far-ranging opinion in *Dred Scott v. Sandford* (1857), Taney declared that the Missouri Compromise had been unconstitutional and that Congress could not bar slavery in the western territories. With Ann driving him (some might say manipulating him), Phillips's disunionist rhetoric became even more strident. It was not so far-fetched as some of his contemporaries believed, however. In a ground-breaking 1978 Organization of American Historians presidential talk, the historian Kenneth Stampp demonstrated that the issue of perpetuity of the Union was not raised at the Constitutional Convention of 1787. The Constitution itself was silent on the question of a state's secession, save that the partition of an existing state would require acquiescence of all the other states.[44]

Garrison had joined Phillips in his disunionist stance. But it certainly rubbed less radical antislavery advocates the wrong way. Phillips and his dwindling crew of admirers were also burning bridges with the Garrisonians over the impact of their agitation. Garrison thought it was bringing over important people to their side. He even hinted at a rapprochement with the

Republicans who favored immediate emancipation (later called the Radical Republicans). Phillips would have none of it and openly attacked Garrison for backsliding. But he would not break with the Garrisonians.

One biographer calls this Phillips's "double vision of politics." The term might also be applied to Phillips's view of national politics. He would not vote or run for office and had never and would never be friendly to organized parties, but he treated both wings of the abolitionists the way that veteran politicians in the two major parties treated the warring wings of their organizations.

The times were rife with plots. Lysander Spooner was back, this time with a plan to raise a Black rebellion in the South. Phillips viewed it the same way that Frederick Douglass would view John Brown's plan—it would never succeed. Philips was watching the abolitionists split into factions, the same way the major political parties were splitting.

It was not that Phillips was incapable of celebration—so long as its object was his vision of an older, purer New England. As he told a Framingham, Massachusetts gathering on July 4, 1859, "It is a glorious country that God has given us, fit in every respect but one to look upon, this holiday of the Union, and seem worthy. . . . Show me such another!" Which Phillips promptly did: "the rotten, shiftless, poor, decrepit, bankrupt South." This was not accurate—certainly not accurate economically, for southern cotton kept New England mills in business.[45]

Unlike Spooner, Phillips did not advocate a violent solution to the problem of slavery until the Civil War erupted. As with his wife Ann and the Weston sisters, his language was radical but his conduct was measured. For example, when he said that the Saxons—white men—had been slaves, he praised the fact that they had been freed by nonviolent means. When Blacks such as Crispus Attucks joined the protest that ended in the Boston Massacre, they proved that race did not matter in the common cause of liberty. Thus, when John Brown came to Massachusetts with a secret plan to liberate the enslaved by raising rebellion in the South, Phillips knew about it but held back his support. Brown's active supporters, the Secret Six—Amos Adams Lawrence, William Lloyd Garrison, Theodore Parker, Thomas Wentworth Higginson, Samuel Gridley Howe, and George Luther Stearns—provided funds.[46]

Brown's raid on the federal armory at Harpers Ferry in western Virginia was a spectacular failure, but Phillips, along with most abolitionists, saw

Brown as a martyr to a divine cause. In a eulogy of Brown on the day of his execution, Phillips prophesized that Brown's actions had begun the end of slavery in the South. At a meeting in Boston on November 19, 1859, Phillips roused the audience with a defense of Brown. Part of that talk was a critique of the Virginia trial of Brown for treason against the state. "That indictment is a rag. It is a net with every thread broken. You might expect it—no blame to [the prosecuting attorney]Mr. [Andrew] Hunter. He prepared it when a whole State was quaking in an earthquake, and had five minutes to do it in. You might have as well asked a man to model a constitution under such circumstances. It is no shame to Mr. Hunter that he has put on record an indictment with rents in it so large that you might drive the whole population of Charlestown through it, and not touch either side [laughter]. Every criminal lawyer knows it." Or, Phillips believed, should have.[47]

His talk was widely reported. Brown, according to Phillips, had acted according to the true American ideal of individualism, according to his own sense of justice and right. Phillips had said the same of himself in his refutation of Spooner. Virginia was nothing more than an "organized piracy," and Brown was justified in sinking it. The *New York Times* added, editorially, that Phillips and his supporters in the audience were not likely to live to see the end of slavery that Brown sought.[48]

. . .

All of this was put to a fiery test in the winter of 1860–61, when South Carolina, followed by six other slave states, announced its intention to depart the Union and establish the Confederate States of America. Phillips, after some soul searching, decided to stand "under the flag" and support military action against the insurrectionists.

CHAPTER 4

Patriot

*O*ver the course of the Civil War, from 1861 to 1865, Phillips turned from a disunionst, demanding that a Union based on slavery be disbanded, to a fierce Unionist. His patriotic turn was genuine, for he saw the war, and the peace that would follow, as the best chance to end slavery and ensure legal equality for the freedmen. The means would be legal reform, a challenge and an opportunity for the nation's lawyers. It was a hopeful prophecy, redolent of the potential of a strong democracy. But first must come obedience to the law, and that meant reversing course on disunionism.

But the war years were an emotional, psychological, and intellectual rollercoaster for Phillips. From urging the dissolution of the Union he became its strong supporter. From refusing to countenance violence he accepted its inevitability and cheered on the troops. He had once praised Seward but then found the secretary of state's change of views abhorrent. Lincoln's caution infuriated him, but Phillips knew that Lincoln was emancipation's best hope. Phillips fired off short pieces to the abolitionist press, gave talks, and attended meetings, but the progress of freedom, and beyond that, of full participation of the freedmen in democracy was agonizingly slow.

. . .

In 52 BCE, Rome's then foremost lawyer, Marcus Tullius Cicero, defended his friend Titus Annius Milo on a charge of murder. The speech he gave

included the now famous aphorism that in times of war, the laws are silent. One might suppose Cicero meant to include the tongues of lawyers.
Nothing could be more wrong about the American Civil War era. The two
sides went to war to defend distinct legal regimes and the social orders
they protected. During the war, rival legal concepts of insurrection (a civil
war within a nation) and belligerency (war between sovereign enemies)
vied for adherents in federal and Confederate councils. Lincoln's cabinet
was replete with lawyers; among them, William Henry Seward, Salmon
Chase, and Edwin Stanton were stalwarts of the prewar antislavery bat-
talion. In Congress, the leadership of the war effort—the senators Sumner,
Benjamin Wade, Zachariah Chandler, and the congressmen Thaddeus
Stevens and George Julian—were all abolitionists. In a "nation of laws,"
such martial legalism was not surprising, no more so than that the nation's
lawyer-politicians—men who went from the practice of law into politics—
found themselves at the center of the maelstrom. That is where Wendell
Phillips placed himself.[1]

The role of Civil War lawyers was not surprising. The leading Republican candidates for the presidency in 1860—Lincoln, Seward, Chase, and
Edward Bates of Missouri—were all lawyers, as were the Democratic candidates Stephen A. Douglas of Illinois and Vice President John C. Breck-
inridge. The last Whig candidate, the former senator John Bell of Tennessee, who ran as an independent, was also a lawyer. As the Union teetered
on the edge of disaster, the electors chose a lawyer to lead the Union in
peace and war. Watching their every move with a critical eye and a sharp
pen was Phillips.[2]

. . .

In almost hypnotic fashion, Phillips was drawn more closely into politics
by this web of politician-lawyers at the center of the crisis. He had never
been a political party player, and did not immediately become one, but
during the crisis and the war that followed his orations turned increasingly to national politics and leading politicians. In 1856, he even took a
leading role in the presidential campaign of John C. Frémont. That was
not surprising, for Phillips was no admirer of Lincoln (incautiously calling him a "slave-hound" at one point), but when the Republicans won the
presidency with electoral votes entirely from free states, Phillips minded
his manners. In a eulogy for his longtime friend and abolitionist ally Theodore Parker, at the Music Hall (where Parker's Unitarian congregation

met), on November 18, 1860, Phillips tried to reconcile his past views with the present situation. He was delighted that Parker's congregation knew no distinction between colors and genders, among rich and poor, making it a perfect example of a democratic public forum. From its pulpit he warned, "One quarter of the community is awake, alive; there is another quarter that pretends to be awake; and the other half are afraid of everybody that is awake." But Phillips was aware of the herculean task that lay before him. "Here we are outvoted; here we are fanatics; and here we are persecuted. But persecution is only want of faith. When a man does not believe what he says he does, he persecutes the man who contradicts him." The future belonged to New England and its reform ministry. "The canvass of the last three months, how valuable it is! You are a canvass every seventh day, and on a higher standpoint, with no necessity to pander to the prejudices or evils of the time."[3]

Phillips's legal advocacy of the end of the Union came face to face with ironic reality when South Carolina led the parade of slave states out of the Union. No sooner was Lincoln elected president than South Carolina's legislature called a secession convention. On December 20, 1860, its members voted unanimously to leave the Union. South Carolina was quickly followed by six other Deep South states.[4]

The secession of the slave states was a surprise to Phillips. At first, he was ecstatic: "Disunion [of the South] leaves God's natural laws to work out their own solution," he announced on January 20, 1861. "The Union is a failure." It was not secession that sparked his words, however, but New York senator William Henry Seward's efforts to preserve the Union—and the slave states in it. Seward believed that time and reason would bring an end to slavery and that the Union was worth saving. Phillips was not mollified. He had already deemed Seward's version of antislavery weak and untrustworthy.[5]

How odd it was, Phillips continued that January, that the agreement with hell that lay at the center of the federal Constitution was excised by the South itself. "This mistake of South Carolina is she fancies there is more chance of saving slavery outside of the Union than inside." Three states had followed, proclaiming their departure. Phillips assumed that all the slave states would follow and "the whole merciless conspiracy of 1787" would be ended. In fact, Maryland, Kentucky, and Missouri would remain in the Union, in part through the efforts of federal troops and military victories. He also assumed that the Confederacy would ask for annexation "on their terms." As of February 17, 1861, he was still advocating letting the slave South go.[6]

In legal terms that would mean some revision of the Constitution. There was (and still is) no mechanism, save force, for secession. As a matter of fact, then, the old Union and the old Constitution could not stand. "Every thinking man sees that, no matter what men wish, it cannot mean the Union as it was. . . . We must change the elements which have created this quarrel, if we would end it. They are only to be changed by emancipation or division." In his speech on the "Dissolution of the Union," on March 21, Phillips had wished for a "peaceful and bloodless emancipation."[7]

That was no longer possible. Later the same year, he would say, "What do I ask of the Government? I do not ask them to announce that policy of emancipation now; they are not strong enough to do it. We can announce it; the people can discuss it; the Administration are not strong enough to announce it." But it must come, he believed. And it must come as a matter of law, not arms, in order to suffice.[8]

.   .   .

As the secession movement gained steam and a countervailing Northern militarism followed, Phillips was left out of the conversation. Bewildered, he pondered how and when to recant his earlier disunionist views. Within three months, Phillips made a complete about-face. He came back swinging; he would not retreat and announced that he welcomed this war. He stood under the flag, urging Lincoln to greater action to end slavery by preserving the Union.[9]

Still, the legal problem remained. When was secession permissible? When could a country declare that a portion of its population was engaged in civil insurrection? The Buchanan administration regarded secession as illegal but decided that the executive had no authority to suppress it. Lincoln agreed that it was illegal, for the Union was perpetual, but at first offered a peace plan to the Confederacy: Do not seize federal property and return to good order, and no penalties would be assessed. He preferred peace to suppression of the rebels. So, too, Phillips explained that his former acceptance of secession rested on his hopes, now dashed, that abolition "cried for peace." But "in the whole of this conflict" he had only one objective—the freeing of the slaves. If only a civil war would produce that outcome, then he was all for vigorous prosecution of the war.[10]

Yet Phillips still did not trust the Republican Party leadership. He never really did. As he revealed on July 4, 1861, "Mr. SEWARD is not honest enough to manage this war; Mr. LINCOLN is not bold enough yet." Phillips did not understand the partnership that Seward and Lincoln were already fashioning. Rivals during the contest for the presidential nomination, they had become trusted allies during the campaign and in the cabinet. In analyzing interpersonal political alliances, Phillips was lost. He would not have fared well in any president's cabinet, but he acutely saw how events had outrun the abilities and the expectations of the nation's leaders. "Neither party—neither the North nor the South—has shown any statesmanship." By "statesmanship," Phillips meant the two sides' (mis)understanding of where the secession movement was going, or at least how far it had gone by the early winter of 1861. "JEFFERSON DAVIS never meant to pass this last Winter out of Washington; [Alexander] STEPHENS never meant that a session of Congress should be held to which he should not be summoned. . . . To-day convicts them of utter lack of statesmanship; for if statesmanship means anything, it means knowing one's times." In fact, both senators had been strong unionists until the final crisis. But they were not the only party leaders Phillips found clueless. "The North, also, has shown no statesmanship; for Mr. LINCOLN thought, and Mr. CHASE thought, and Mr. CAMERON thought, that the South would never dare to secede; that South Carolina was not mad enough to try the gulf on the edge of which she stood." The only concession to reality came at the end of the talk: "We all miscalculated our times in a most important point and degree."[11]

Phillips's assessment of the political crisis was not far off the mark, but whatever the incapacity of the politicians, as a legal matter, no law allowed secession. If Phillips said this outright, he would be implying that his own oratory of the past twenty years was sheer hypocrisy. A legal positivist to the core, believing that existing law must be obeyed, he had concluded that the only way to defeat immoral law was to depart that legal system altogether. His could not escape his own logic. He had wanted out of the Union. He wanted the Constitution quashed or revised. What irony, then, that South Carolina had followed his prescription. The South Carolina secessionists who met in convention and voted—the republican prescription for legal change—had feared that Lincoln and the Republicans would do what Phillips and other abolitionists had demanded and make slavery illegal. Thus, the only recourse for the slave South was to leave the Union.

The inconsistency with his past attack on the Constitution now pointed its finger at him. He knew it, and to ignore it or deny it would have been foolhardy. "Some friends criticize me because I seem to them to have surrendered my favorite plea of disunion, and welcomed this war. . . . I have advocated disunion for fifteen years, because I thought it a practicable and peaceable method of freeing the North from the guilt of Slavery, and of planting at the South the seeds of early and entire emancipation—wringing justice from a weak and bankrupt South. But it has pleased the Nation to seek that result in a different way." This clever, one might say legalistic, turn of argument enabled Phillips to escape the contradiction between his previous and his present stances on disunionism: he had always, he now averred, "starting with the principle that this was a Nation, not a partnership, have constantly claimed that the corner-stone of our Government, the spirit of '76, was the full liberty of each and every human being." The Constitution was flawed. The revolution and the Declaration of Independence were pure. The proof was the election of Lincoln, a mirror of the act of the Revolutionaries. After all, only a few years after celebrating the coronation of George III, the colonists voted for independence. Phillips compared his volte-face with theirs; Lincoln was now "the picket and outpost of the great Abolition army, taking quarters in the Capitol." Despite Phillips's own preference for a peaceful resolution to the slave problem, "twenty millions have chosen otherwise. . . . Hence I bow to the masses, and welcome emancipation by war." Setting aside the military language, bowing to the masses, was another way of expressing strong democracy.[12]

Phillips would have preferred "peace and argument," whatever that meant, to ending slavery with rifles and cannons. But over the years, peace and argument had proved nothing, provided nothing, changed nothing. In what domain of life would one prefer peace and argument to other means? The answer was that in law, peace and argument were the only means of resolution. Before secession, Phillips had offered peace and argument to take the free states out of a Union whose Constitution protected slavery. Now that peace and argument had failed in that effort, war was the remaining option. But did war mean that law had no place in the great endeavor of ending slavery? For Phillips, the very opposite was true. He wanted to make the war not for the Union, but for the end of slavery—by law. "It seems to me that there is but one way of developing a Union sentiment in those Southern States, and of subduing the secession sentiment equally, and that is, by arraying a might of power, and putting behind it a purpose, that shall remove the cause that makes us two people. That is, not until you call four million of blacks into liberty."[13]

In his speech of July 4, 1861, Phillips acknowledged his continuing astonishment at the spread of secessionism, but not his own volte-face. "What can I say to you to-day? No man can feel himself particularly competent to make a speech on the Anti-Slavery question just now." Rather than rejoicing that the work of abolition was finally gaining momentum, he hesitated. "It is all guess-work. The only question is, whether it is probable one man will guess a little better than another."[14]

But now he was hopeful. "I feel satisfied that the end of the slave system has come. I have no doubt that we begin to touch the end." He, who put so much stress on words, now relied on actions. "The age of discussion is over. We have had fifty years, more or less, of what is called agitation, discussion and party divisions. Now, a new act has opened. It is the hour of fight—the age of bullets. That never lasts very long. It does not take as much time for a nation to fight itself clear as it does to talk itself clear." But his prediction on this, as on so much that had gone before, was inaccurate. He assumed, as did much of the free North, that the South would soon be brought to heel—just as the Confederacy assumed that a few victories would convince the North to leave the South alone. "I do mean to say this, that the South has fully come to the conviction, that unless she can use the Union to support Slavery, the system is gone; and I think the North has come to this conviction, that the Union never shall be used to sustain Slavery." Had he a better grasp of politics, he might have foreseen how divisive the party system in the North would be, and how resilient the increasingly one-party Democratic South would be, but then few national politicians understood what the election of Lincoln would bring. "I think, so far, the public mind is made up . . . that the Union either does or shall mean liberty in the end. Those two ideas conflict—hence the war. We are in it; how shall we get out of it?"[15]

At the July 4, 1861, gathering he promised the crowd only a few words, then proceeded to offer a major speech. His words flowed forth like a flood bursting levees and could not be contained. He reached into the commonplace book he had been compiling since his early adulthood and added to it a commentary on current events. "There are only two ways by which a nation is molded. One is by its great men; the other is by its masses. We have not been brought to this spot by what we called our great men; we have been brought here by our masses." This was pure strong democracy; the war was the will of the people. Although at least for the present, the war was relatively popular in the North (that would change with defeats on the battlefield), in fact the war was the work of the politicians. There was no plebiscite, no referendum. Lincoln assumed that the majority of Southern opinion was unionist. He might have been right, but the men at the eleven states' secession conventions did not represent the will of the majority. The loudest voices were the ones that were heard. In the North, had another election followed the 1860 poll, the voters might well have opted for continued negotiation and concession. But there was no poll. Over time, the masses would weigh in with their bayonets, but that was in the future.[16]

Although the Constitution forbade such a policy of forced emancipation (the position that the former Supreme Court justice Benjamin Robbins Curtis, an old foe of Phillips, took in 1862, after the Emancipation Proclamation was announced), Phillips declared, "Even fair play to Liberty, under the old Constitution, will be such a change as will quell the South and educate the North. If Gen. [Robert] PATTERSON knows no better than to suppress servile insurrections, cashier him on this side the Potomac. The Administration can, should, ought, if it means liberty, indicate its purpose by these legal, constitutional and imperative measures." Phillips did not expect this to happen, however. Again, he was wrong.[17]

Still, he was willing to backtrack a little. "I want to take back that name which I endeavored to write on the forehead of ABRAHAM LINCOLN, of Springfield—'the slave-hound of Illinois;' and, instead of it, before the first day of January, 1862, I want to write on that same honored brow, 'Liberator of four million bondmen; first President of the free United States of America.'" Phillips called on this audience to "help him to that fame. The Western lawyer is 'willing,' only he has not the courage to offer. [Laughter.] We can help him. Help him by the Press." In other words, he summoned public opinion to help Lincoln endorse universal emancipation. To this end, Phillips offered words, his most generous and his only gift. But he took back what he offered as soon as he said it. "For myself, I put no value on the Union. It is a name—nothing more. It is a parchment, stained and bloody. It were enough for me to damn it forever, that THOMAS SIMS and ANTHONY BURNS bear witness against it on the pavements of Boston."[18]

. . .

Hailed in wartime for views that had gotten him mobbed a year before, Phillips returned to the lecture circuit. Avoiding direct criticism of Lincoln's administration, he lectured in Washington, DC and throughout the (then) Northwest. He even ventured into slave country—Kentucky. But after a year of war, Phillips's exasperation at the prospects for emancipation had only grown. In August 1862, he told one audience, "I think the present purpose of the government, so far as it has now a purpose, is to end the war and save slavery. I believe Mr. Lincoln is conducting this war, at present, with the purpose of saving slavery."[19]

When the administration, led by Lincoln and Seward, proclaimed emancipation, Phillips was again caught wrong-footed. He should have celebrated, but he had not anticipated it, and he did not see its impact. Moreover, he did not apologize for his lack of foresight. Nevertheless, Phillips welcomed the Proclamation. In a January 9, 1863 article for the the *Liberator*, he praised Lincoln for attacking the "entire system" of slavery. That was not entirely accurate, at least reflecting Lincoln's ideas. Lincoln had never been an abolitionist. He pursued emancipation reluctantly. Thus, the Lincoln historian Eric Foner finds Phillips's views legally wanting, for the Proclamation only applied to slaves in rebel hands. More would be necessary to render slavery unlawful.

Although this is narrowly true, Phillips's pronouncement was truer in a larger sense. The proclamation said, for the first time, officially, that the highest authority in the nation found slavery repugnant and unlawful, and that the slaves taken from their insurrectionist masters were and would be forever free. Horace Greeley's *New York Herald* agreed with Phillips, calling it a "watershed" from which there was no turning back. But for Phillips, the Proclamation was not enough.

On August 8, 1863, the *New York Times* reprinted a Phillips letter to the *Liberator* "DEAR SIR: You ask me how we, who have hitherto been disunionists, now join in supporting the Union. I answer: 'our effort to break the Union was only a means to an end. Our object was the abolition of Slavery.'" He continued, more than a little disingenuously, "Let me remind you that we never undervalued Union—never had any objection to Union—but only to a Union on Pro-Slavery conditions, one that supported and strengthened Slavery." The ideal Union was one in which all the people participated in self-government. That meant that "slavery . . . [must be] immediately repudiated at every cost." Phillips merely and consistently looked for a "direct and efficient way of educating the public to a stern Anti-Slavery principle."[20]

Phillips followed his own logic to its extreme conclusion. "We sought such disunion for the slave's sake." However, leaving the fate of the enslaved in the hands of a Confederate nation composed entirely of slave states would hardly lead to the end of slavery. Even if the severing of the Union into free and slave regions were possible (as in fact the Confederacy wanted), the overall prospects of the enslaved would only be worse. Phillips conceded as much, for "we know also that our plan would leave the slave to struggle up to freedom against a thousand obstacles, alone and unaided, vexed and hampered by a reluctant master." But no longer having the taint of slavery in the North's nostrils would be better than futile attempts to aid the enslaved in the existing Union under the present Constitution. One had to swallow hard to accommodate this reasoning, but Phillips's gullet was exceptionably flexible.[21]

One might defend Phillips's logic by concluding that disunionism was the only truly positivistic solution to the problem of slavery for an abolitionist. But if secession from a Union that permitted slavery were constitutional for the North, then surely it was defensible for the slave South to protect slavery, as Phillips almost conceded. If that were so, then the federal government had no legal recourse within the Constitution to force secessionists back into the Union. In fact, Phillips had said so in 1861.[22]

Once again, Phillips reversed the course of his reasoning; or rather, he replaced rationalizations with narrative: "War came. The South began a war on the nation. To accept disunion then, one not begun by an Anti-Slavery North, but forced on a reluctant and half-converted North, though it would have killed Slavery in the end, would have lost the slave his share in the nation he helped to found, and would have left the slave obstructed in his path to freedom by great obstacles, unpitied, unaided, vexed and hampered by an embittered master." Even in retrospect, it is almost impossible for the historian to parse the argument here. The causal connections are so tangled that one can only conclude that Phillips's letter was a version of his ad hoc manner of public speaking, taken down by a befuddled secretary at the *Liberator*. But the conclusion he drew from his analysis was clear enough.

"Such disunion, too, would probably have helped to prolong Slavery" had it not been challenged by the federal government. "The first gun the South fired gave the nation the constitutional right to abolish Slavery wherever its flag floats, showed that such a measure would inevitably be necessary, and that the Union must probably cease, or rest on the equal liberty of all races." "The equal liberty of all races" was the key phrase in the letter. It was nothing more or less than a rephrasing of strong democracy.[23]

Phillips added the last part of his doctrine to his letter. He was less concerned with justifying his 180-degree turnabout on the issue of disunion than with his shift on the use of violence. The law must be obeyed—that was basic positivism. The Confederates had violated the law. They must be punished. Phillips had not advocated slave rebellion, though he gave support to those who did. But now he advocated violence on a much broader scale. "In these circumstances, the Abolitionists, who were not peace men, and had never asserted the sinfulness of war, perceived that the war itself would produce an overwhelming national opinion adverse to Slavery sooner than any other agency." To Phillips, the connection to loyalty was obvious. "The manifestation war must make of the nature and designs of the Slave Power, would inevitably make every Unionist an Abolitionist."[24]

Whatever the accuracy or the potency of Phillips's vision, he clearly was engaging in what the historian Michael Les Benedict has called "constitutional politics."[25] The essence of that politics was a rule of law, an idealized version of Massachusetts law, compared with the injustice of Southern law. As Phillips wrote for the *Liberator* on the first day of 1864, true victory for the Union must be cemented in law—amendments to the Constitution ending slavery forever, where it existed, and guaranteeing equal protection of the law to all, whatever their race or previous condition of servitude. For the formerly enslaved to participate fully, they must have the right to vote. For that vote to be an educated one, they must have schools and teachers. Phillips's vision was farseeing—envisioning the Civil Rights Acts, the Fourteenth and Fifteenth Amendments, the Freedmen's Bureau, and reparations (still debated in the twenty-first century). "We never shall have a nation until it is governed by one idea. The idea of Massachusetts liberty is MANHOOD; a human being, not an artificial being; a thing created by God, not by law. The Southern idea of liberty has been, a white race lifted into position by law, and a black race thrust down into its position by law. The idea of Massachusetts liberty is, a man competent to sell his own toil, to select his own work, and, when he differs with his neighbor, a jury to appeal to."[26]

As 1864 opened, Phillips found Lincoln too weak and the emancipation process incomplete. Phillips understood that the Emancipation Proclamation freed slaves only in places still in rebellion, and that was not enough. As he told an audience at the Women's Loyal National League, reported in the *New York Times* on February 16, 1864, "The rebellion had killed Slavery, but killed it as a typhus fever kills a man who rises at length from his bed and drags a weary life of pain for a half dozen years and then dies. When it would die no one knew; that depended upon the statesmanship of the future upon the method of reconstruction." About that he was certainly right. In a far more sweeping claim, he envisioned a very different America after slavery. "We are not again to see the nation in which we were born. The old-fashioned calm, quiet, home-bred, school-house farming Republic is gone forever." Although his vision was far ahead of its time, he was right about the danger to the Constitution in postwar America. "A million of disbanded soldiers, half fit for war, half unfit for anything else, will be scattered among us. They are to bring back to civil life ten thousand officers, their idols. . . . That same military bias and spirit has been the grave of free government in all time. On the other side we are to have that other great danger to free government, an immense debt." The *Liberator* of February 26, 1864, reported a conversation between Phillips and Garrison in which Phillips declared that either [Lincoln] must be "CRUSHED INTO SUBMISSION" to all of his (Phillips's) views, "or we must have a different leader for the next four years."[27]

However, like Lincoln's, Phillips's thinking was still rooted in the "old" Constitution. That is, both men assumed the weakness of the federal government relative to the power of the states. This was not quite the states' rights ideology of St. George Tucker and John C. Calhoun, but it was the rule of constitutional interpretation that many political leaders shared at the outset of the war. In this sense, then, Phillips was a states' rights advocate. He had long thought that Massachusetts's antislavery law superseded federal proslavery law. This was one reason he could argue for the dissolution of the Union and not be an anarchist (unlike some of the more radical abolitionists). As he told a Boston audience in 1864, after learning of Lincoln's Proclamation of Amnesty and Reconstruction, with its proposal to reconstruct the states when 10 percent of the former Confederates had taken loyalty oaths to the Constitution: "Why, we have put up a fence between the Federal Government and the State Government. The bill before the House proposes, for instance, that South Carolina, with 300,000 white men, and not a loyalist among them, and 400,000 black men, and not a disloyalist among them, shall be reconstructed, the fence erected between us and them, the government of the State given to these 300,000 rebels, and the black men put under their feet helplessly." This was because the federal government, under the "old" Constitution, regarded state sovereignty as impregnable. "Put up the fence between you and Louisiana or South Carolina, and the Federal law runs to it, not over it, except in two or three specified cases."[28]

He saw the lenience of Lincoln's reconstruction plan for Louisiana and shuddered. He also had a vision of constitutional amendments being driven from the field by a phalanx of white Southern racists, who would use violence to undo law. Phillips's positivism, with its obedience to law, revealed its full implications here. The white South must obey the proposed Thirteenth Amendment. "I allow, of course, what every man knows, that all this time we had a pro-slavery public: we are to have an anti-slavery one, I hope, in the future; but I want to bring to your minds, first, the almost impossibility, even with the Constitution on our side, of attacking a State, and then to remind you that the white men of the reconstructed States can keep inside the Constitution, be free from any legal criticism, and yet put the negro where no Abolitionist would be willing to see him."[29]

Phillips hoped that the answer to this dire prospect was to give freedmen the franchise. "I fall back on the democratic principle, and claim of the anti-slavery party that it shall be content with no emancipation which does not put into the hands of the freedmen himself the power to protect his newly-acquired liberty (applause). No emancipation is effectual, no freedom is real, which does not take that shape." Were Phillips truly prescient and aware of the fatal illogic in his argument as well, he would see that the same forces that denied equality to the freedmen could use cunning and violence to take the vote from them. Phillips's jurisprudence of strong democratic positivism was a dream that would not become reality until a hundred years later.[30]

But Phillips dared to dream. Indeed, in the opening phases of the Civil War, Phillips had laid out his vision of a strong democratic positivism as though it were inevitable. "We come here to recognize the fact that, in moments like these, the statesmanship of the Cabinet itself is but a pine shingle on the rapids of Niagara, borne which way the great popular heart and the National purpose direct." The command of the state was the expression of the popular will. "Our object now is to concentrate and to manifest, to make evident, and to make intense the matured purpose of the nation." In time of war, as in peace, the state must be obeyed, so long as it was a representative of the people's will. "What I claim is, in honor of our institutions, that we are not put to the alternative of the carnage of a General. Our fathers left us with a such pliant, miserable Government. They gave us a Government, with the power, in such times as these, of doing anything that would save the helm of State in the hands of its citizens." This was as far from John Austin's *Principles of Jurisprudence* as one could get, but Phillips had been working out the kinks for many years. At the core of his strong democratic positivism was equality. "Some men say they would view the war as white men. I condescend to no such narrowness. I view it as an American citizen—proud to be a citizen of an Empire that knows neither black nor white—neither Saxon nor Indian—but shelters all under a sceptre, equal and impartial over all." That vision persisted in his oratory throughout the war. If one sets aside his patriotic bluster, the vision was clear. "I acknowledge the great principle contained in the Declaration of Independence, that a State exists for the liberty and happiness of the people." All the people.[31]

Phillips's view of strong democratic positivism took practical form closer to home. For example, in a speech advocating a city police force for Boston, he applied the doctrine to crime in the city. He had considered the reforms in London, New York, and other cities, and declared that "it is one of vital importance to the welfare and progress of our city, and, until the object be achieved, it can never be too frequently considered and urged." He had seen the destructive potential of the urban mob at first hand, but the issue was not merely the protection of abolitionist speakers. In fact, something of the reverse was true. "The experience of all great accumulations of property and population reads us a lesson, that the execution of the laws therein demands extra consideration and peculiar machinery." The enslaved were property—did he mean that property in enslaved persons had to be insured? Had he forgotten that the Emancipation Proclamation was the greatest expropriation of private property in the nation's history? (Recall that it applied to territories still in rebellion, not to enslavers in rebellion.) The model was not a broad one, however, but a far narrower one—the judiciary. "We put the interpretation of the laws—the judiciary—not into the hands of any local municipal body, but the interpretation of the State laws is in the hands of persons appointed by the whole State." Reform of local problems should not be based on public opinion or local democratic voting but on professional, expert authority. How often had Phillips challenged that authority when it required the return of runaways to their enslavers? But fidelity to law here reasserted itself in his thinking, calling up the impartiality and training of the lawyer. "The era of public opinion is finished, that of law has commenced. . . . The era of discussion and opinion is over; the era of legislation has come—the time when the minority sits down and obeys."[32]

. . .

Phillips's remarks on the crime question may be read as pure Austinian positivism rather than strong democratic positivism, but they corresponded to his plans for Reconstruction. In a series of contributions to the *National Anti-Slavery Standard* in mid-spring and summer 1864, Philips laid out his plan for Reconstruction. It focused less on the return of the seceding states and the repatriation of the rebels than on the rights and privileges of the newly freed. They were to have an education, land, and the right to vote. Some of these goals came to pass, at least in the days after the collapse of the Confederacy, first by private individual efforts, then by the Reconstruction amendments to the federal Constitution. But Phillips's conception of the problem and its solution lay firmly in antebellum ideas, not in the institutional innovations of wartime. Freedom for the formerly enslaved meant that they would be able to seek the same opportunities as their white neighbors. Reconstruction would elevate and liberate, but that was all. It was then up to the freedmen to seize the opportunities.[33]

For reasons that are not entirely clear to this day, Phillips made the wartime secretary of state, William Henry Seward, a target of his vitriol. Denounced by his political opponents as a rabid abolitionist, Seward was something quite different. His view of slavery was rooted in a philosophy of relational rights. Slavery denied to the enslaved his rightful part in the community, the reciprocity and hospitality on which all human rights rested. Seward attacked slavery when he was the governor of New York and in the Senate. However, he was also a strong Unionist and tried, until the final crisis, to find a way around secession. This infuriated Phillips. Seward's active use of his wartime power to confine, investigate, and punish Southern sympathizers during the war also angered Phillips. The reason he gave was that the suspension of the writ of habeas corpus and the military trials of Copperheads (pro-Confederacy Northerners) raised serious problems with strong democratic positivism. The wartime prosecution of Confederate sympathizers might be necessary, but basic rights in a democratic republic were at stake in the North: "To-day, Mr. Chairman, every one of them, habeas corpus, the right of free meeting and a free Press are annihilated in every square mile of the Republic. We live to-day, every one of us, under martial-law or mob law. The Secretary of State [Seward] puts [suspected dissenters] into his bastille." Phillips could not resist criticism of Seward, long a target, but then he backpedaled: "Mark me, I am not complaining. I do not say it is not necessary. It is necessary to do anything to save the ship." But he worried that "we are tending toward that strong Government which frightened JEFFERSON, and toward that unlimited debt, that endless army." It was an odd choice of models—Jefferson was an enslaver—but Phillips was trying to defend two very different positions. "Understand me, I do not complain of this state of things; but it is momentous. I only ask you that out of this peril you be sure to get something worthy of the crisis through which you have passed." That "something" was his other, older cause—the permanent end of slavery.[34]

Phillips's complaint with Seward did raise genuine issues, but he put it aside for a time. On November 8, 1864, after the presidential election had returned Lincoln and Republican majorities in both houses of Congress, with the future demise of the Confederacy all but certain, and the draft Thirteenth Amendment having passed the Senate, Phillips addressed the Boston Anti-Slavery Society's annual meeting. He was no longer the beleaguered spokesman for an unpopular cause. Antislavery was the law of the land. He now presented a fuller version of his strong democratic positivism. If the law was the will of the people as embodied in legislation, it must and should be obeyed. He told the gathering, "The future just opening upon us has one question for abolitionists, and that is, the terms of reconstruction. The great danger in that future consists in three facts. The first is, that the prejudice against the negro is not more than half eradicated from the North. Secondly, that the republican party, which has the Government in its control, is weakened in its principle by the very numbers which have rallied to its flag. Thirdly, that the Executive pleads earnestly an immediate reconstruction of States, within the next twelve months." The Thirteenth Amendment was not sufficient to guarantee to the freedmen all that Phillips understood they deserved in a strong democracy. A full array of legal reforms was required and must be enforced. "Now, to my mind, an American abolitionist, when he asks freedom for the negro, means effectually freedom, real freedom, something that can maintain and vindicate itself." The guarantor of that freedom was statutory protection, but even more important, the right to vote guaranteed by law. "I fall back on the democratic principle, and claim of the anti-slavery party that it shall be content with no emancipation which does not put into the hands of the freedman himself the power to protect his newly-acquired liberty."[35]

Phillips was not happy with the progress of the Thirteenth Amendment through Congress or with the efforts of the executive branch to gain passage of the amendment. The new Congress would not take be seated until the end of 1865, and the debate through the winter of 1864–65 evidenced how tired the wartime members were. Democrats opposed to the amendment cited it as evidence of a plan to destroy the sovereignty of the states and prevent genuine reunion. A few of these politicians played the racist card, declaring that the amendment would lead to the eventuality of black equality, plunging the nation into the depths of miscegenation. Even without this claim, racism was a central theme of the Democratic opposition to the amendment. Racism rejected any claim that free or freed people of color had to have equality before the law. Republicans replied by lauding the heroism of the Black Union soldiers, but except for a few genuine radicals such as Charles Sumner, stopped short of promising the full panoply of civil rights for the freedmen. Democrats still insisted that the amendment would be an unconstitutional enlargement of the powers of government. Republicans replied that state legislatures would have the final say, conforming to the original intent of the framers. Repeatedly, Lincoln interceded personally, a moment captured in Steven Spielberg's prizewinning movie *Lincoln*. Seward was now even more active, organizing a lobbying campaign to gain the votes of New York Democrats.[36]

But what would that new regime of law look like? And who was to fashion it? Phillips, who had heretofore stood on the sidelines of electoral politics, during the war felt compelled to enter the game. His political sense was hardly better in the waning days of the war than it had been at its inception, however. He angered the moderate Republicans, infuriated the centrist union Democrats, and even lost favor among the radicals when he publicly broke with Garrison. The two men had strong personal ties and shared much ideological ground, but Phillips's persistent support of Frémont over Lincoln estranged them. Phillips's attacks on Lincoln, even after he won a second term, derived from Lincoln's relative conciliatory attitude toward the rebels and his tepid support of the Thirteenth Amendment—tepid at least in Phillips's eyes. Garrison's own zeal for the common cause was not so strong as it had been. When on May 9, 1865, Garrison called for the dissolution of the American Anti-Slavery Society, claiming its mission had been accomplished, the breach between the two men widened.[37]

CHAPTER 5

Elder Statesman

hough never accorded the honorific of elder statesman, for he had eschewed a role in government, during the Reconstruction era after the Civil War, Wendell Phillips became exactly that. His contribution to the end of slavery was secure; his vision of the new world after slavery was prophetic. If Reconstruction, in the words of its foremost historian, was an "unfinished revolution," few in either North or South at the time shared that judgment. Phillips was an exception. His postwar vision of strong democracy encompassed inclusion and equality of race and gender.[1]

. . .

For the majority of Republicans in Congress, Reconstruction was not a revolution, but a series of necessary reforms undertaken episodically. For Lincoln, at least at first, and his vice president (later president), Andrew Johnson, and more so after 1865, it was a restoration. Lincoln's plan for amnesty and pardon was first offered to the Confederacy in 1863, and again in his message to Congress in 1864, after his reelection. Whereas Lincoln's last speeches welcomed the political participation of the freedmen, after his assassination Johnson and the Democrats adamantly opposed enfranchising them.

Meanwhile, Republicans in Congress labored to insure the freedmen some of the benefits of their emancipation, passing the first of a number of civil rights acts. The congressional elections of 1866, following a year of

violent attacks against Blacks in the South, gave Republicans the impetus to pass the Fourteenth Amendment and impose it on the recalcitrant
Southern states. This "Congressional Reconstruction" constitutionalized
protection of civil rights. The Fifteenth Amendment barred states from
denying the franchise on the basis of color or former condition of servitude but did not extend this right to women. Nor did it prevent private
actors from undermining the purpose of the reform.[2]

Phillips was in accord with the new civil rights laws and the new Thirteenth, Fourteenth, and Fifteenth Amendments. He spoke out against
those who did not recognize the strong democratic potential of Reconstruction. After April 1865 he could no longer target Lincoln for failing to
fulfill his ideals, but William Henry Seward remained in office at Johnson's side. Comparing Seward's view of Reconstruction with Phillips's
shows how revolutionary Phillips's view was.

Restoration was the theme of Secretary of State Seward's only formal
address on the question. On February 22, 1866, at the Cooper Institute in
New York, Seward gave his last full public statement on the treatment of
the freedmen and-women. In response to the invitation, he pled his own
exhaustion but could not refuse to give the George Washington Birthday
Address where Lincoln had spoken six years earlier. He was sanguine. "The
union—that is to say the nation—has been rescued from its perils." The
greater portion of the job was done. What remained was not nearly so important as what he and Lincoln's administration had achieved. The rest
was "merely a difference of opinion" about the restoration of full relations
between the former Confederates and their countrymen. Questions such as
these were always "worthy of deliberate examination and consideration."

Seward did not subscribe to the radical Republican agenda. Race relations must be worked out within communities of people who lived and
worked together, not imposed by Congress. Slavery was gone, without
compensation; secession was gone, without recrimination. "I apprehend
no serious difficulty or calamity" from the controversy between the president (Andrew Johnson) and the majority of Congress. Loyal men from
the now loyal states stood and waited while Congress passed law after law
and imposed "burden after burden" on them. When they were readmitted
to Congress, the job of restoration would be complete. The issue then
outstanding—the Freedmen's Bureau, renewed by Congress in 1866 but
vetoed by Lincoln's successor, Johnson—was "unimportant."[3]

Seward, a lawyer himself, reflected the attitude of the many lawyers who served the two sides in the war. Now demobilized, Union and Confederate lawyers played a vital role in bringing the nation together after the Civil War, however. They did this by returning to the core business of lawyering—bringing and defending lawsuits and representing clients in dispute resolution. Georgia's Howell Cobb had served as a member of the US Congress, governor of Georgia, president of the provisional Congress of the Confederacy, and then as a general in the Confederate army. He reopened his law office and reported to his wife in December 1865 that the first fees had arrived: "If constant attendance and close attention to business will bring in more we shall get it." Alexander H. Stephens, another former member of the US Congress and then vice president of the Confederate States of America, was no sooner released from custody than he returned to practice in the state court circuit in Georgia. When the fuller normalization of relations came with the reopening of the federal courts in the South, he practiced in federal court. The signatures of former Confederate members of the bar accompanying their oaths of allegiance were duly recorded by federal district court clerks in the records books—some signatures in bold hands, some frail and barely legible. At the same time, the lawyers' return to their offices and the courtrooms was good *for* them. Prewar racism returned but took new forms. As soon as these "distinguished" Southern lawyers take oaths of loyalty than they prepared the black codes that all but re-enslaved the freedmen after the war. But now newly minted African American lawyers fought these black codes in the courts.[4]

Phillips watched with concern as the former rebels returned to their law practices. Rather than a revolution, the end of the war brought back to power the supposedly moderate, sensible men who had opposed emancipation in the first place. Now they said, Go slowly on Black rights. They agreed that in demanding full legal equality for the freedmen, Philips was "fighting windmills." Relax, they urged him, the battle is won. As Henry Raymond, a moderate Republican and antislavery (not abolitionist) founding editor of the *New York Times* explained, "If the question of negro suffrage can be left to the calm action of considerate and responsible men, it can be adjusted without substantial difficulty, and in accordance with the best interests of the negro race and of the whole country. The main point is already settled; the negro is no longer a slave—he is a man, and he will have accorded to him, in due time and in full measure, all the political rights and privileges which are enjoyed by other men under the same circumstances."5

.   .   .

Unhappily tied to the tail of the radical Republican wagon, alienated from many old colleagues, Phillips's op-ed pieces in the *National Anti-Slavery Standard* bounced wildly. As an editorial writer he had a platform for public interest lawyering, but his contributions lacked the coherence and impact of his antislavery orations. He made concessions to the party, followed by recantations of those concessions. He even hazarded fortune by running for the Massachusetts governor's office in 1870 as the Temperance and Labor Reform Party candidate (he did not win). In the meantime his old target, "rebeldom," grew stronger as the radical impulses of the North weakened. He blamed Andrew Johnson for violence in the South but had little influence even when the Republicans won a decisive victory in the congressional contest of 1866. Violence in Louisiana had once again inspired Phillips to call for suppression of the white South. The resulting acts of Congress seemed to come from Phillips's pen. But the struggle against the racialist legacy of slavery was not won.6

Still, the triumph of arms released Phillips from his earlier constraints to explain what strong democracy would really be: Massachusetts. Massachusetts troops, in particular the Fifty-Fourth and Fifty-Fifth Massachusetts Regiments (colored infantry) were raised and trained in his home state. His former bodyguards, among whom were Harvard College undergraduates, had also greatly contributed to the victory. "They cohere by the school house, a common lineage, a common language, common books, common associations, common habits of labor, invention, and ingenuity." How this was possible with the diversity of ethnicities and religions in America was not clear—apparently strong democracy rested, at least when Phillips was happy, on something like the anticipation of New England as a future pluralistic society.7

Yet for Phillips, Reconstruction seemed to move in jumps. Progress was punctuated and imperiled by elections, a political evolution whose uncertainties and reactions deeply concerned him. As "editorial writer" on the *National Anti-Slavery Standard,* he commented dryly and cynically on the motives of the two parties. His pieces in the paper were strongly worded but not very original.

For example, he found the election of 1866 was stained by President Johnson's betrayal of the Radical Republican program. Congress had lost his trust by not conferring the franchise on the freedmen. Phillips could do nothing about a laggard Congress, but he called on it to impeach and disqualify Johnson. "We say to Congress, impeach the president, or share the infamy to which history will consign him." It was not a bad prediction, as events would prove. Though Phillips's attachment to the Republican Party endured, he believed that the draft Fourteenth Amendment was a victory for the former Confederates and their Democratic allies rather than for the freedmen. It was framed in the negative, rather than as a positive grant of rights. What the formerly enslaved had gained by the victory the politicians were throwing aside. "It needs no future hours to show that [Congress] has broken the nation's pledges to the loyal men of the South as well as the former bondmen." Phillips's biographer James Brewer Stewart argues that here and elsewhere, Phillips was developing a concept of "nationality" whose centerpiece would be the defeat of the watered-down Fourteenth Amendment and instead the guarantee of land, education, and the vote for the formerly enslaved. Land ownership would raise the freedman to the same status as the white American yeoman farmer; education would insure that the freedman could take advantage of his freedom; and the vote would guarantee protection against the violence of the former Confederates.[8]

In 1868, the Republicans nominated the former US Army commanding general Ulysses S. Grant of Ohio for the presidency. Grant won. Phillips was pleased. Unlike Johnson and the Democrats, Grant took enforcing Reconstruction seriously. Throughout the South, extralegal violence had denied to Blacks, whether formerly enslaved or formerly free, the rights that the Fourteenth Amendment and the Civil Rights Act of 1866 had formally conferred. With a strong majority in the Congress, Grant adamantly punished Southern anti-Black violence. His message to Congress, on March 23, 1871, said: "A condition of affairs now exists in some of the States of the Union rendering life and property insecure, and the carrying of the mails and the collection of the revenue dangerous. The proof that such a condition of affairs exists in some localities is now before the Senate. That the power to correct these evils is beyond the control of State authorities, I do not doubt. That the power of the Executive of the United States, acting within the limits of existing laws, is sufficient for present emergencies, is not clear." Congress passed and Grant signed a series of powerful civil rights laws, the so-called Enforcement (Force) Acts, between 1870 and 1871. These criminal statutes protected the freedmen's right to vote, to hold office, to serve on juries, and to receive equal protection of the law. Most important, they authorized the federal government to intervene when the states did not act. Promoted by Grant and his attorney general, Amos T. Akerman, the strongest of these laws was the Ku Klux Klan Act. Signed by Grant on April 20, 1871, it authorized the president to impose martial law and suspend the writ of habeas corpus.[9]

Phillips's approach to the problem of white Southern resistance (called "Redemption") was different, reflecting his adherence to strong democracy. At the dedication of a memorial to Elijah Lovejoy, Phillips repeated that the struggle would never be over, or won, until the white man and the Black man stood on equal footing. That was the simplest formulation of strong democracy and the most potent. It was why Lovejoy's sacrifice remained worth remembering. All the promises from Washington, DC would not accomplish this, for they had no more weight than paper. Absolute equality in all phases of life, lived every day, was the only true guarantor of victory. Ironically, in this sense Phillips's strong democracy and Seward's relational rights converged. Only when the freedmen were fully part of integrated communities could real equality exist. Phillips's advocacy of reparations for slavery, appearing in the 1870 *National Anti-Slavery Standard,* included all these notions. In many ways, it anticipated the modern reparations argument. "The whole nation recognizes the fitness and necessity of securing land to the Negro." Voting rights and other civil rights were incomplete without economic rights. He proposed that the federal government lend the freedmen money to buy tools, land, farm animals, and seed. The problem of course, one that Phillips seemed not to understand, was that southern agriculture had long since passed the stage of self-sufficiency. It was market driven, and control of that market was not in the hands of the small producer. How was the freedman to pay back the loan? The entire system of postwar agriculture depended on access to continuing finance, distant markets, and the cultivation of staple crops. Throwing the freedmen back into the precommercial era was unrealistic, as proven by the rise of sharecropping. In this, as in his view of women's rights and workers' rights and temperance, Phillips was still wedded to prewar notions of society.[10]

Phillips's "Negro's Claim" speech set strong democratic positivism at the very center of Reconstruction. Coming as it did in 1870, context meant everything. Everything for which the un-Reconstructed South fought the war had come undone. Phillips drafted his speech just a few weeks prior to the ratification of the Fifteenth Amendment, which states, "The right of citizens of the United States to vote shall not be denied or abridged by the United States or by any state on account of race, color, or previous condition of servitude." But like its predecessors, the amendment fell short of a guarantee that all citizens could vote, however, women not least. More important, it was directed to government agencies, and thus did not protect potential voters against private violence as they attempted to vote. Although a second clause gave to Congress the power to "enforce this article by appropriate legislation," that power seemed to be limited to the action of the federal and state governments. Still, the vote was what Phillips had wanted so that the freedmen could protect themselves.

. . .

Why not then rest on his laurels, like William Lloyd Garrison, now that the prime objective was achieved? Garrison announced that victory was won. For Phillips, who engineered the continuation of the American Anti-Slavery Society over Garrison's objections, victory was not yet certain. Strong democratic positivism did not rest on one cause but on a broad array of causes. His continued advocacy of workers' rights, women's rights, and temperance had antedated the war. In one sense, he was simply being consistent. In his 1840–41 travels in Europe, Phillips had been horrified at the disparity between great wealth and extreme poverty there. He had joined in the Saratoga Springs movement for women's equality. These causes were never separate from his abolitionism. More important, by the end of the war, the means—strong democratic positivism—had become the end of his public interest lawyering. Only when all men and women could claim full civil rights and liberties would those rights be safe for anyone.

Like his ideas of yeoman farmers, Phillips's conception of working-men was rooted in older Jacksonian ideals of independent producers. Although he was a favorite speaker at workingmen's meetings, he never did quite grasp how factory labor differed from the older artisanal work model. Thus, his advocacy at times seemed antique, or at least out of phase with the new industrialism. "I am a Democrat, a Jacksonian Democrat, in the Darkest hour." Under strong democratic positivism, the law should protect the workingman against the abuses of the capitalist and protect the capitalist from the abuses of the workingman. Ideally, the worker and the capitalist could then cooperate. "We all know there is no war between labor and capital; that they are partners, not enemies." Although this shows a naiveté about class structure as well as politics, Phillips's notions of free labor without slavery were consistent with his opposition to slavery. Ending monopoly, allowing the free exchange of labor for wages, educating the workingman, and ensuring voting rights for all became his watchword. He assumed that the workers themselves would accomplish this reform regime: "It is the working masses who are really about to put their hands to the work of governing." Perhaps this is why he had not looked very far into the inequities of Lowell many years earlier.[11]

When Phillips's advocacy of women's rights continued into the postwar period, where it faced two crises. First, at its center, as in his speeches on labor, was the importance of political participation. It was logical, and for him imperative, to give women the vote, alongside workers and freedmen. No one need fear the state or its laws, for all the people would make those laws. In an 1859 speech he had made that plain. "What, then, do we claim? We claim that woman should vote. . . . Woman does her full share in forming the mind of the age; we only ask that she should have a direct influence at the ballot-box and in civil affairs." Strong democratic positivism would be democratic only when women took part; otherwise laws made for them by others that they had to obey were the same abuse as slavery. This realization was the fundamental principle on which the authority of the civil state rested.[12]

But unlike the slavery question and worker's rights, the "woman question" had to be argued against the opinions of some women. As he told a New York audience in 1866, "The slave stood behind us," and labor joined the crusade for better wages and working conditions, but "woman is herself the obstacle" to her liberation and her equality. Not all women, of course. for Phillips worked in close accord with Susan B. Anthony and Elizabeth Cady Stanton, among others. Women's concession to their own submission betrayed a sense of inferiority that history and plain fact belied. Women ruled in private life, why not in public affairs? Their "unrecognized influence must be turned to open . . . power." But here, as in the early days of abolition, public opinion seemed against him. How could he argue that strong democratic positivism required women's franchise when the majority of women seemed opposed, when the "prejudice of men" blinded them? The answer lay in educating women in their own cause. Throughout his public interest lawyering, Phillips proposed that the law should be obeyed when it rested on public opinion, but public opinion had to be shaped. Strong democratic positivism had become his goal rather than his means.[13]

Second, when after the war the project of the franchise for the newly freed was at stake, Phillips waffled in his advocacy of the franchise for women. It was a matter of priorities. He recognized that including it in legislation or an amendment to the federal Constitution might fatally weaken similar efforts to enfranchise Black men. His former allies, such as Stanton and Anthony, were infuriated. Later historians have taken repeated the accusations of Elizabeth Cady Stanton and Susan B. Anthony. For example, Faye Dudden has read this controversy as an example of white male patriarchy: "Wendell Phillips's patrician self-confidence was such that he felt justified in telling activist women what to do, and when Stanton and Anthony refused to defer, he used underhanded methods and denied them funds to which they were entitled. By the middle of 1866, Stanton and Anthony had been forced to create a new organization devoted to the simultaneous agitation of black and women's rights, the American Equal Rights Association." When he opposed (and defeated) their attempts to put the Anti-Slavery Society behind women's voting rights, arguing that women did not need the vote to influence public life, they turned their guns on him. He replied by personal testimony of his attachment to feminism and attempted to defuse the confrontation by going on tour to rally support for Black voting. In the meantime, many leading female reformers either deserted the Anti-Slavery Society or openly condemned its policies.[14]

But the "Negro Hour" came first. Phillips's ideal of equality was naive but powerful: "Social equality follows hard upon the heels of the ballot box." Well, perhaps not so naive, for he suggested that "the South knows this." Democracy in the white South followed the expansion of the franchise in the Jacksonian era, when the white yeoman farmer and farm laborer could cast ballots alongside their economic betters. But the glue of this faux equality had always been the belief that rich and poor whites always stood above the slave. Would this same elevation by voting apply when whites and Blacks stood side by side on voting lines? Phillips assumed that the war, and the participation of black troops, made the real lesson of the war was "that there was no distinction of races." For Phillips, that precept became a prescription to "ignore all races." In effect, the whole of the nation was now the antislavery society. Some Republicans, such as Thurlow Weed of New York, undermined this ideal and the party that had won the war by seeking their own advantage in splintering the party. The constitutionalists in the Republican Party, who harked back to the precedents of 1860, did not see how the war had revolutionized the Constitution by bringing "the absolute equality of every person before the law." Again and again, conservative Republicans in Congress wavered, Democrats obstructed, and the Supreme Court balked at the project of full equality for the freedman. So to the women of the reform movement, who protested their exclusion, he pleaded "to every woman who knows its value by the injustice done her," to work diligently for the suffrage of the former bondmen."[15]

Phillips's view of immigration and immigration law integrated all these themes. It showed the breadth of his vision as well as its limitations. The question concerned limiting the flow of Chinese into the country, and for those already in the country, limiting their rights. The dilemma would end with the Chinese Exclusion Act of 1882, but that narrow and bigoted legislation still lay in the future when Phillips's editorial appeared in the *National Anti-Slavery Standard* on July 30, 1870. Phillips proposed that "we welcome every man of every race to our soil and to the protection of our laws. We welcome every man to the best opportunities of improving himself and making money that our social and political systems afford. Let every oppressed man come; let every poor man come; let every man who wishes to change his residence come,—we welcome all; frankly acknowledging the principle that every human being has the right to choose his residence just where he pleases on the planet."[16]

Phillips's ingrained New England elitist racial essentialism here emerged. It had already stained his view of the enslaved. "This brings us to the question of importing Chinese laborers. The Chinese are a painstaking, industrious, thrifty, inventive, self-respectful, and law-abiding race. They have some pretentions to democratic institutions and moral culture,—are a little too many machines; but we shall soon shake that servility out of them." All the Chinese, bundled together into one race? But for him the higher law of individual choice was more important than the imposition of older New England values. "Their coming will be a welcome and valuable addition to the mosaic of our nationality; but, in order to that, they must come spontaneously, of their own free-will and motion, as the Irish, Germans, and English have done." Now he added his free labor assumptions. The danger was the degradation of the Chinese into enslavement: "If the capital of the country sets to work, by system and wide co-operation, to import them in masses, to disgorge them upon us with unnatural rapidity,—then their coming will be a peril to our political system, and a disastrous check to our social progress." Thus the solution was to treat the Chinese immigrant as a candidate for full admission to republican citizenship. "We lay it down as a fundamental principle,—never to be lost sight of,—that every immigrant of every race must be admitted to citizenship, if he asks for it. The right to be naturalized must not be limited by race, creed, or birthplace." This individualizing process would be protected, as it was by the Fifteenth Amendment for the freedmen, by the franchise. "Every adult here, native or naturalized, must vote." The solution was not just assimilation, however. It was legal. "We hold it to be clearly within the province, and at clearly the duty of legislation, to avert this danger."[17]

Phillips, no doubt influenced by the Boston Clique, was a strong supporter of temperance. In 1851, Maine passed a law prohibiting the production and sale of alcohol. Massachusetts followed suit. After the first version was declared unconstitutional by the Massachusetts high court, a revised bill passed into law in 1855. Boston was having none of it, however, and its city government resisted. In his February 1865 address on the liquor laws to the state legislative committee, Phillips avowed the same legal positivism. It did not matter to him whether those laws were sound or not. Those who opposed them should try to change them in conventions, with elections, and in the legislature. Until then, however, they must be obeyed. He was not going to argue on this occasion for temperance. That cause (in which he believed) had been argued long enough. Boston, however, was waging a campaign of willful resistance. Did that sound familiar? Did it not resemble the abolitionists' long campaign against the fugitive slave laws? No matter. If the law had public opinion on its side, then obey it. "All we claim is that, when [Boston] is beaten in the court of law, they obey it." He had a new adversary here: "the criminal classes, banded together, rich, massed up, are too strong for democratic institutions." He did not mean street thugs but the liquor interests and their allies in the city government. Thus the enemy of democratic law was corruption—a theme familiar to all who studied politics in the 1850s.[18]

· · ·

In 1879, Phillips's longtime collaborator, friend, mentor, and abolitionist icon William Lloyd Garrison passed away. Though in later years somewhat estranged from Garrison, Phillips knew his debt and partially paid it at Garrison's funeral. It was a chance for the aging Phillips, now sixty-eight years old himself, to reflect on what the two of them had accomplished and what remained for the next generation. Both men had championed the abolition of slavery, women's rights, and other causes. But in 1865 Garrison had declared victory, whereas Phillips had seen a long road ahead to full equality for all. "This hour is for the utterance of a lesson . . . especially in the hearing of these young listeners, who did not see that marvelous career." Garrison had begun the "agitation" that would slay slavery. This was true enough, but Phillips was recognized as the real agitator, for he did it in front of angry crowds. Here began Phillips's attribution to Garrison of what Phillips himself wanted to be remembered for. "Fastened on that daily life was a malignant attention and criticism such as no American has ever endured." Yet "no man, however mad with hate, however fierce in assault, ever dared to hint that there was anything low in motive, false in assertion, selfish in purpose, dishonest in method,—never a stain on the thought, the word, or the deed." And throughout it all, "what American ever held his hand so long and so powerfully on the helm of social, intellectual, and moral America?" And in course of time, it showed that "fewer mistakes in that long agitation of fifty years can be charged to his account than to any other American. Erratic as men supposed him, intemperate in utterance, mad in judgment, an enthusiast gone crazy, the moment you sat down at his side, patient in explanation, clear in statement, sound in judgment."[19]

CHAPTER 6

The Duty of a Scholar in a Republic

*P*hillips's failing powers were evident in the speeches of his final years. He still traveled and lectured, but it was more for the remuneration than for public interest causes. Published collections of his earlier speeches had already appeared, but they could not duplicate his galvanizing sense of his audience and his conversational delivery. Typically, on January 24, 1881, Phillips delivered a formal address refuting the arguments of one Chancellor Crosby, at the Methodist Episcopal Church in Boston, on the subject of temperance. He read from a manuscript, something that he had rarely done in past years. The noteworthy part of the refutation was that he returned to legal positivism—this time in an exploration of the legislative process. For the democratic positivist, legislative action is the purest expression of the authority of the state. That was one reason that Phillips spoke so consistently for women's right to vote and for the Fifteenth Amendment. When the legislature truly represented the will of the people, statute law was the people's law. But it was a weak performance, lacking his customary vigor of argument and variety of references.[1]

. . .

Thus, the alumni of the Phi Beta Kappa chapter of Harvard College thought twice about asking him to give the keynote at the honor society's centennial celebration. But his reputation and status won out. Given the chance to bring together the threads of his advocacy in a single address, a kind of valedictory, he agreed. The result was his Harvard College Phi Beta Kappa Centennial Anniversary keynote speech on June 30, 1881. He titled it "The Duty of a Scholar in a Republic." One can only suppose that he was the scholar in question, in his own mind at least, but the talk was messy, free-associating entries in his notebook, bits and pieces from his personal experience, and comments on the state of education. In earlier addresses, his sense of purpose had pulled together the whirling universe of his thoughts. Now they flew in all directions, as if by centrifugal force. The opening passages exemplified the rest. "Though a linguist should pride himself to have all the tongues that Babel cleft the world into, yet if he had not studied the solid things in them, as well as the words and lexicons, he were nothing so much to be esteemed a learned man as any yeoman competently wise in his mother dialect only." Think things, not words—a sound admonition, even before it was disseminated by Oliver Wendell Holmes Jr. eleven years later—but ironic from a man whose career was words. Trust the ordinary, not the learned, again ironic from a man so well schooled, from birth, in learning.[2]

From Milton, to Aristotle, to Disraeli, to the Spartans his thoughts flew. He had hesitated to accept the invitation, and it is easy to dismiss the speech as the product of old age and weakening powers. But a thread ran through it that held together all of his thinking—or rather two threads, woven at opposite ends of the cloth. He longed for a day of gentlemanly thought gone by, lamented the shortfall of the reforms he championed, and wished that there was some way to bring together the fragments of the higher learning. It was as if a precursor of the five-foot book shelf of *Harvard Classics* (1909) assembled by Charles W. Eliot and John Eskine of Columbia University's Western Civilization course collapsed together into Phillips's lap. Then he tossed the old classics aside and championed the common sense of the masses.[3]

One finds one's way through Phillips's rambling with some difficulty. There are familiar waystations, however. He argued that excellence was a New England virtue. And there was a nationality of democratic thought. "Mr. President and brothers of the P. B. K.: A hundred years ago our society was planted,—a slip from the older root in Virginia. . . . No matter how much or how little truth there may be in the tradition; no matter what was the origin or what was the object of our society, if it had any special one,—both are long since forgotten. We stand now simply a representative of free, brave, American scholarship."[4]

The elite Phillips had emerged from a slumber of decades of radical advocacy, blinking his eyes and shaking his head, as if the great events of his own day had not happened. "In one of those glowing, and as yet unequalled pictures which [Edward] Everett drew for us, here and elsewhere, of Revolutionary scenes, I remember his saying, that the independence we then won, if taken in its literal and narrow sense, was of no interest and little value; but, construed in the fulness of its real meaning, it bound us to a distinctive American character and purpose, to a keen sense of large responsibility, and to a generous self-devotion." Everett came from the same Brahmin stock as Phillips. Phillips's parents would have been proud. He honored his, and their, forebears. "The first generation of Puritans . . . included some men, indeed not a few, worthy to walk close to Roger Williams and Sir Henry Vane,—the two men deepest in thought and bravest in speech of all who spoke English in their day, and equal to any in practical statesmanship. Sir Harry Vane, in my judgment the noblest human being who ever walked the streets of yonder city,—I do not forget Franklin or Sam Adams, Washington or Fayette, Garrison or John Brown,—but Vane dwells an arrow's flight above them all, and his touch consecrated the continent to measureless toleration of opinion and entire equality of rights."[5]

Henry Vane was a young man when he came to Boston, where he supported the radical ministers John Cotton and John Wheelwright in the Antinomian controversy. Vane was briefly governor of the colony, and then went back to England, leaving his allies in the controversy, including Anne Hutchinson, high and dry. Why did Phillips find in him "the pure gold of two hundred and fifty years of American civilization, with no particle of its dross"? The answer was that Vane was a statesman as well as a religious figure, and a supporter of tolerance (of a limited sort) in a time of religious warfare and persecution. "He stands among English statesmen preeminently the representative, in practice and in theory, of serene faith in the safety of trusting truth wholly to her own defence." In other words, he did not compromise his principles, and when it appeared that he would lose, he did not submit, but shed power and left. He was, thus, a model for Phillips, who did not compromise his principles. "Vane's ermine has no stain; no act of his needs explanation or apology." As it happened, Vane also had a hand in the founding of Harvard College.[6]

Phillips's historical account was by turns unforgiving and celebratory, a contrarian quality typical of his own life. He condemned the "narrowness and poverty of colonial life" when the pure light of Vane was extinguished in the colonies as in England, corruption and luxury. But virtue could not be entirely suppressed, and "industry and a jealous sense of personal freedom obeyed, in their rapid growth, the law of their natures." That law was mirrored in "English common-sense and those municipal institutions born of the common law, and which had saved and sheltered it, grew inevitably too large for the eggshell of English dependence, and allowed it to drop off as naturally as the chick does when she is ready." The process was not a radical one. "There was no change of law, nothing that could properly be called revolution, only noiseless growth, the seed bursting into flower, infancy becoming manhood." In old age, the radical had become the Whig, for there is no purer example of the Whig theory of history than Phillips's celebration of 1776.[7]

Slavery was missing from this short account of colonial history—why is a mystery. This was Phillips's chance to condemn Harvard (and the Royall family, whose generosity to Harvard College was enormous) for its part in the slave trade—or at least to revive the claims that Thomas Jefferson had made in the Declaration of Independence against George III for encouraging the slave trade. They were easy targets. Perhaps the reason for his reticence was that such a judgment would fall on Phillips's own ancestors as well. Phillips's view of history was a personal kind of recapitulation theory: the growth (phylogeny) of the nation mirrored the growth (ontogeny) of the individual. "When the veil was withdrawn, what stood revealed astonished the world. It showed the undreamt power, the serene strength of simple manhood, free from the burden and restraint of absurd institutions in Church and State." Phillips's version of this biogenetic theory was, of course, a metaphor, but perhaps applied to his own growth. His manhood was reflected in the triumphant rise of nation.[8]

It also was odd that Phillips, who had spent so much time tracing the history of his own family and of New England, would turn his back on the discipline of history. He was candid. "When I was a student here, my favorite study was history. The world and affairs have shown me that one half of history is loose conjecture, and much of the rest is the writer's opinion." Now his reversal of position was sweeping. "History is, for the most part, an idle amusement, the daydream of pedants and triflers.

The details of events, the actors' motives, and their relation to each other are buried with them." Academic history was especially useless. "Yet, we complacently argue and speculate about matters a thousand miles off, and a thousand years ago, as if we knew them." Then came the reason for his confession. "Any one familiar with courts will testify how rare it is for an honest man to give a perfectly correct account of a transaction." No lawyer should trust the history coming from the mouth of an interested party, a witness, or a deponent. Facts may be forthcoming from such sources, but "when you come to men's motives and characters . . . [they] make all [history's] records worthless." He had seen how politicians twisted facts. He had seen how judges disregarded facts. He did not say, but surely those of his generation knew, that judges and politicians had not treated the abolitionists kindly.[9]

At least law itself could be half trusted. "Standing on Saxon foundations, and inspired, perhaps, in some degree by Latin example, we have done what no race, no nation, no age, had before dared even to try. We have founded a republic on the unlimited suffrage of the millions. We have actually worked out the problem that man, as God created him, may be trusted with self-government. We have shown the world that a Church without a bishop, and a State without a king, is an actual, real, every-day possibility." Good laws had done this. "A hundred years ago our fathers announced this sublime, and, as it seemed then, foolhardy declaration, that God intended all men to be free and equal: all men, without restriction, without qualification, without limit."[10]

Forgetting the admonitions against historical memory and accuracy he had issued a few moments previously, he concluded, "A hundred years have rolled away since that venturous declaration [of independence]; and to-day, with a territory that joins ocean to ocean, with fifty millions of people, with two wars behind her, with the grand achievement of having grappled with the fearful disease that threatened her central life and broken four millions of fetters, the great Republic, stronger than ever, launches into the second century of her existence." Apparently, history did matter: "The history of the world has no such chapter in its breadth, its depth, its significance, or its bearing on future history."[11]

Phillips's historical lesson was leavened with his ethnic prejudices, though he had warned against histories seen through the prejudices of the observer. He did not credit that the Anglo-Saxon view of history was a prejudice, however. "Their serene faith completed the gift which the Anglo-Saxon race makes to humanity. We have not only established a new measure of the possibilities of the race; we have laid on strength, wisdom, and skill a new responsibility." Note that he had shifted from third person to first person: "we." At the same time, the "attempt of one class to prescribe the law, the religion, the morals, or the trade of another is both unjust and harmful." No wonder that his audience was by this time entirely confused. He extolled the extension of the franchise to all people, then returned to a noblesse oblige: "Power, ability, influence, character, virtue, are only trusts with which to serve our time."[12]

Back and forth, through all the themes of his own life, the prejudices and the aspirations of his class, and the history of the nation he went. "We all agree in the duty of scholars to help those less favored in life, and that this duty of scholars to educate the mass is still more imperative in a republic, since a republic trusts the State wholly to the intelligence and moral sense of the people." He followed this credo of the elite with the exuberance of the democrat: "The experience of the last forty years shows every man that law has no atom of strength, either in Boston or New Orleans, unless, and only so far as, public opinion indorses it, and that your life, goods, and good name rest on the moral sense, self-respect, and law-abiding mood of the men that walk the streets, and hardly a whit on the provisions of the statute-book." Phillips's assault on the bench and bar of Massachusetts was already well known. But a rejection of law itself, though he had spent a lifetime calling for better laws or at least changes in laws, went beyond mere cavil. "Easy men dream that we live under a government of law. Absurd mistake! we live under a government of men and newspapers. Your first attempt to stem dominant and keenly-cherished opinions will reveal this to you."[13]

Then back he went to singing the praise of the plebs, to which he added a plea for a more hands-on education. Who did not admire the "ideal Yankee, who 'has more brains in his hand than others have in their skulls.'" One has to remember that universal education was one of Phillips's long-standing goals. For a graduate of Harvard College and Harvard Law School, that commitment may seem odd, but Massachusetts was the home of the public school movement. Horace Mann, the first secretary of the state board of education, saw compulsory, universal, free public education as a patriotic and an economic goal. Mann wrote, "Education must prepare our citizens to become municipal officers, intelligent jurors, honest witnesses, legislators, or competent judges of legislation." Surely Mann's recognition of the demands of a democratic legal positivism should have appealed to Phillips. The references to law were appropriate. Mann was an abolitionist, and while a congressman had defended two men accused of "stealing" seventy-five slaves. (He, and they, lost) But Phillips, who strewed famous names around like an assistant professor at an academic sherry hour, never mentioned Mann. The reason is no mystery. Mann, who had "a fiery temper," had blasted Phillips in an 1853 *Liberator* contribution. The result was a "wrestling match of controversy" between the two Massachusetts luminaries over whether a true abolitionist could hold office (Mann) or not (Phillips).[14]

In any case, Mann's subject was elementary education. Harvard College's curriculum was anything but elementary. The kind of education Phillips meant was education for life, a cross between vocational school and preparation for holding public office. "In this sense the Frémont campaign of 1856 taught Americans more than a hundred colleges; and John Brown's pulpit at Harpers Ferry was equal to any ten thousand ordinary [academic] chairs." Phillips had supported Frémont's campaigns for the presidency and Brown's raid on Harpers Ferry. Scholars contemned Brown and ignored Frémont. "The book-men, as a class, have not yet acknowledged him." But the "people's schools" taught what the book-men scorned, for "timid scholarship either shrinks from sharing in these agitations, or denounces them as vulgar and dangerous interference by incompetent hands with matters above them."[15]

In much the same way that he often had harangued the proslavery men in his audiences, Phillips told an audience of "book-men" and their students, "Trust the people—the wise and the ignorant, the good and the bad—with the gravest questions, and in the end you educate the race." Although all the lessons the elite might learn from the masses were "not necessarily good ones," nevertheless, "Men are educated and the State uplifted by allowing all—every one—to broach all their mistakes and advocate all their errors." The freedom of speech that the beleaguered abolitionists so treasured was essential to American strong democratic positivism. Participatory public life was the only guarantee of freedom.[16]

Then Phillips returned to the law for an example. "In boyhood and early life I was honored with the friendship of [John] Lothrop Motley. He grew up in the thin air of Boston provincialism, and dined on such weak diet. I remember sitting with him once in the State House when he was a member of our legislature. With biting words and a keen crayon he sketched the ludicrous points in the minds and persons of his fellow-members, and tearing up the pictures, said scornfully, 'What can become of a country with such fellows as these making its laws? No safe investments; your good name lied away any hour, and little worth keeping if it were not.' If law made by the representatives of the people was untrustworthy (in the literal sense of the word) what could one expect of the people themselves? Nothing? Everything!" Motley "went to Europe; spent four or five years. I met him the day he landed on his return. As if our laughing talk in the State House had that moment ended, he took my hand with the sudden exclamation, 'You were all right; I was all wrong! It *is* a country worth dying for; better still, worth living and working for, to make it all it can be!'" Ralph Nader could not have told a more apposite anecdote. Nor would one have been more appropriate for a public interest lawyer. The people must be educated, but once educated, were the best rulers.[17]

Scholars and book-men, aristocrats and autocrats, all shared in "the growing dislike of universal suffrage." For a parallel reason, "the white South hate[d] universal suffrage" as did the "so-called cultivated North." Another example, again from the law: "[The former US attorney general William B.] Evarts and his committee, appointed to inquire why the New York City government is a failure, were not wise enough, or did not dare, to point out the real cause,—the tyranny of that tool of the demagogue, the corner grog-shop; but they advised taking away the ballot from the poor citizen." Corruption did not come from the bottom, but from the head. As the railroad mogul Jay Gould put it, "It is cheaper to buy legislatures."[18]

· · ·

Here, then, was Phillips's formula for a strong democratic positivism. Do not simply obey the command of the state. Ensure that the state is truly worth obeying by ensuring that it is truly democratic. And ensure democracy by universal franchise. But fear of true democracy was widespread, so cautions must be provided. "It is not the masses who have most disgraced our political annals. I have seen many mobs between the seaboard and the Mississippi. I never saw or heard of any but well-dressed mobs, assembled and countenanced, if not always led in person, by respectability and what called itself education."[19]

Phillips was not exaggerating. He had been heckled in Ohio and threatened in Massachusetts. He had employed bodyguards. He knew the danger was real. "No wonder the humbler class looks on the whole scene with alarm. They see their dearest right in peril. When the easy class conspires to steal, what wonder the humbler class draws together to defend itself?" For Phillips, the dearest right was not just the vote, however. It was the First Amendment right to speak. Voting was a form of public speech, and expansion of the franchise was essential to the protection of speech. For suppression of speech was "the next move." Like any lawyer, Phillips turned to a hypothetical. "Suppose that universal suffrage endangered peace and threatened property." Antislavery speech had done just that, and both mobs and laws—the two sides of the antebellum slaveocracy's coin— sought to muzzle the abolitionists. But freedom of speech was the mother of all rights. "To ripen, lift, and educate a man is the first duty. Trade, law, learning, science, and religion are only the scaffolding wherewith to build a man." In other words, all elite culture rested upon a plebeian foundation, the arts were epiphenomena. "Despotism looks down into the poor man's cradle, and knows it can crush resistance and curb ill-will."[20]

Free speech knew no class or status. "I urge on college-bred men, that, as a class, they fail in republican duty when they allow others to lead in the agitation of the great social questions which stir and educate the age." Agitation—the use of speech to call out injustice—belonged to all men. "Agitation is an old word with a new meaning. Its means are reason and argument,—no appeal to arms." Agitation stirred the conscience and awakened the intellect. Then the people might "Wait patiently for the growth of public opinion. That secured, then every step taken is taken forever. An abuse once removed never reappears in history." Agitation was the watchword of the public interest lawyer. Agitation in the court of public opinion was the surest form of public interest. "The agitator must stand outside of organizations, with no bread to earn, no candidate to elect, no party to save, no object but truth,—to tear a question open and riddle it with light."[21]

Phillips selected a familiar example to prove the case: "The crusade against slavery—that grand hypocrisy which poisoned the national life of two generations—was one." In the course of that conflict, "Every great issue, civil and moral, was involved,—toleration of opinion, limits of authority, relation of citizen to law." Censorship, the burning of books, the murder of those who exercised their right to free speech, were all part of the conflict.

But out of the maelstrom came glimmerings of reform. Again, Phillips had an example ready to hand. "For forty years plain men and women, working noiselessly, have washed away that opprobrium; the statute-books of thirty States have been remodeled, and woman stands to-day almost face to face with her last claim,—the ballot." When "summoning woman into the political arena" was a reality, free speech would triumph. For, Phillips declared, "I know what reform needs, and all it needs, [is] a land where discussion is free, the press untrammeled, and where public halls protect debate." Then and only then, "In such a land he is doubly and trebly guilty who, except in some most extreme case, disturbs the sober rule of law and order." So, at the end stood the agitator and the lawyer, one and the same.[22]

The Lost Arts

*I*n public, Phillips was reserved. His words might be fiery; he was not. Part composure, part restraint, this self-imposed distant demeanor kept him from becoming a beloved figure like Garrison. He remained the gentleman born and bred. For him, slavery was almost an abstraction—an evil surely, but not one with which he was personally acquainted. This lack of intimacy was characteristic of his participation in other causes, for example his deafness on the woman question in 1866 and his inability to understand what working people really wanted. He traveled widely but never to the slave South or to the precincts of the poor. He was a man for the people, but not of the people.

All those contradictions are not obstacles to an appreciation of his contribution but opportunities to see behind the public mask. In Boston Brahmin society, material gain and public obligation were intertwined. In a class whose duty was an ever-present burden, self-esteem was essential to the integration of public and private lives. Phillips strove to bring these two parts of that experience together in a way that protected his self-esteem. Or rather, his self-esteem helped him prove to himself and to others that he was worthy of his family heritage. He did not choose his father's route—through public office. He did, however, engage in charitable works to an almost obsessive degree. Linking those traits to his lecturing, one sees how they fulfilled the needs of self-esteem. Strong self-esteem

often manifests in adherence to principles. Even in the face of strong opposition or difficulty, trust in one's own opinions and course of action
and resistance to criticism will carry the day. All of these traits describe
Phillips, as his correspondents recognized in him.[1]

Self-esteem, or as Phillips customarily described it, self-regard, did not
rest on winning law cases, besting opponents in the arena of the courtroom, or obtaining large legal fees—some of the conventional measures of
success in legal practice. Self-esteem came from hewing to the course of
duty without deviating from knowing that one was right whatever others
might say. It was living a life of duty. It was confidence without arrogance.
For example, when not speaking before a crowd, Phillips was self-effacing
and modest. In a culture of conscience, what mattered most was how he
regarded his own conduct. He was the epitome of a guilt-based culture,
as opposed to a shame-based culture, in which how others see one is one's
measure of self.[2]

When we admire someone, we often see in them what we would like to
see in ourselves. As we have seen, on May 28, 1879, Phillips offered a eulogy of his comrade William Lloyd Garrison. He declared that Garrison's
life was "a grand example" of the rule that "we have no right to be silent"
when we see injustice. This was the outgrowth of Garrison's own "moral
nature . . . unaided, uninfluenced from outside." Though his eulogy of
Garrison, Phillips was surely writing about himself. Whose "unfailing
courage" did Phillips celebrate? Not just Garrison's, but his own. So,
too, when Phillips eulogized his longtime friend Charles Sumner, that is
what stood out for him about Sumner: "He never retreated a step, never
turned a hair from the right path, never took back a word." Phillips's ability to channel these basic needs into the quest for justice for others not so
blessed by birth and pedigree as he is a measure of his greatness.[3]

.   .   .

We live in a time when law and legal ideas have once again taken center
stage in our national news. Judicial decisions on a wide variety of public
and private issues affect us all. Legal commentators have joined the judges,
law professors, and practitioners in trying to explain (defend and criticize)
the decisions. The period of Phillips's public life offered a similarly contested landscape of law—when slavery and freedom, rights and privileges,
race and gender were all subjects of public debate. Into this maelstrom
he went, armed with righteous fervor, broad education, and the gift for

speaking in public. What is more, and most important here, he pioneered the craft of public interest lawyering based on a jurisprudence of strong democratic positivism. Do we—should we—share his outrage, his frustration at the stubbornly lingering legacies of antebellum injustice?[4]

This brings us to the very same dilemma that constitutional theory faces today. Should a Constitution "conceived in original sin" be worthy of obedience? The disguising of a proslavery document by eliding the word *slave* was but one of the framers' delicts. May not one argue that the federalists of 1787 so blatantly and hypocritically misrepresented the Constitution to the Indigenous peoples that it cannot be honored? In its duplicity—promising white elites that the federal government would eliminate the Indian threat and simultaneously promoting the new government to Native Americans as protection for their rights—the taint of the document continued well into the twentieth century. Such exclusion was not unique to Native Americans. But for many modern commentators, the Constitution "both justified and came to stand for a legal system built on racial exclusion and violence." Such a taint might never be "redeemed." Phillips would not have agreed, however.[5]

. . .

One lecture that Phillips gave by popular demand over a thousand times from 1838 to 1884 was "The Lost Arts." For many Americans who heard it, and many who heard of it, the talk was closely associated with the man. In his final presentation of this lecture, in 1884, he spoke in a wistful vein. "Ladies and Gentlemen: I am to talk to you to-night about 'The lost arts,'—a lecture which has grown under my hand year after year, and which belongs to that first phase of the lyceum system, before it undertook to meddle with political duties or dangerous and angry questions of ethics; when it was merely an academic institution, trying to win busy men back to books." Phillips looked back at his own career, and in particular his lectures. "Well, I have been somewhat criticised, year after year, for this endeavor to open up the claims of old times. I have been charged with repeating useless fables with no foundation." But to him the lesson was plain, criticized on not. "In every matter that relates to invention, to use, or beauty, or form, we are borrowers." And the lesson Phillips borrowed from history was simple: the great ones "created a public opinion, and unity of purpose." His methods—well, his agitation—was "voluntary, public, and aboveboard."[6]

Effective abolitionism—abolitionism that had a chance to end slavery and gain for the former slave full citizenship—had to be a public opinion crusade. The same was true for every long-shot minority rights cause that Phillips championed. Bad law made inequality and abuse possible and profitable. Bad law divided people by color and class and gender. These were not natural and certainly not just distinctions. Still, bad law must be obeyed until public opinion changed bad law into good law. It was all a matter of law. Inveigh against the evils all reformers might, but without a change in public opinion they cried out in vain. Moral and religious arguments did little but comfort the reformer. Only a revolution in law would solve the problem of inequity. Only a revolution in law would lead to a new regime of civil rights and civil liberties for the formerly enslaved. As Phillips said at the outset, and again in the closing act of his public life, "Above all, plant yourself on the millions. The sympathy of every human being, no matter how ignorant or how humble, adds weight to public opinion."[7]

Phillips's own likely answer to the tainted Constitution argument bears repeating in this context. Lawyers have a duty to speak out against injustice, not just to serve their clients. Public interest lawyering takes the discourse of justice beyond the paper barrier of constitutional text into the real world of harms. The public interest lawyer becomes the nation's conscience, ending constitutional silence. But ultimate triumph of public interest lawyering for Phillips rested on his vision of a strong democracy. Only in it and with it could the command of the state—legal positivism—be fulfilled.

Acknowledgments

$\mathcal{W}$here I teach, the University of Georgia Libraries are the subscribers to or the owners of a remarkable set of online historical sources, including Accessible Archives, African American Periodicals, African American Newspapers, America's Historical Newspapers, the Hathi Trust Digital Library, and the *New York Times* Historical Full Text, among others. All have been greatly useful. I wish to thank Douglas Egerton, Paul Finkelman, John David Smith, and Mark W. Summers for reading the manuscript. Their comments were exceedingly helpful. Ted Rossier, Keith Dougherty, Jeremy Kingston Cynamon, and the members of the American Founding Group at the University of Georgia commented on the introduction and chapter 2 and raised important questions. N. E. H. Hull and Williamjames Hull Hoffer offered stylistic assistance, as they have in previous projects. I cannot thank them all enough. At Kent State University Press, Clara Totten was a model acquisitions editor. Barbara Curialle's copyediting was superb.

Notes

1. Quotations from Irving Bartlett, "Wendell Phillips and the Eloquence of Abuse," *American Quarterly* 11 (1959): 509–20; James Brewer Stewart, "Comfortable in His Own Skin: Wendell Phillips and Radical Egalitarianism," in *Wendell Phillips, Social Justice and the Power of the Past*, ed. A. J. Aiséirithe and Donald Yacovone (Baton Rouge: Louisiana State University Press, 2011), 111–32.

2. Not only do the major biographers slight the impact of Phillips's formal learning in the law but some able students of the "Boston Clique" to which Phillips belonged simply ignore the fact that he was a lawyer. See, for example, Lawrence J. Friedman, *Gregarious Saints: Self and Community in American Abolitionism, 1830–1870* (Cambridge: Cambridge University Press, 1982): "after [Samuel E.] Sewall left, [Ellis Gray] Loring, Nathaniel Peabody Rogers, and [Edmund] Quincy were the only lawyers in the Clique" (46). Only one Phillips scholar correctly notes how rooted in the law and in legal thinking was his own position: Dean Grodzins, "Wendell Phillips, The Rule of Law, and Anti-Slavery Violence," in Aiséirithe and Yacovone, *Phillips*, 89–110.

3. James Redpath, "Biographical Sketch of Wendell Phillips," in *Speeches, Lectures, and Letters of Wendell Phillips*, 2nd ser. (Boston: Lee and Shepard, 1894), iii.

4. "Strong democracy" is a term coined by Benjamin R. Barber in his classic work *Strong Democracy: Participatory Politics for a New Age* (Berkeley: University of California Press, 1984), 4. It means that the ideal state is one in which everyone participates. Phillips did not adopt this term, but he did adopt the ideology. For remaining quotations in this paragraph, see William Wiecek, *The Sources*

of Anti-Slavery Constitutionalism in America, 1760–1848 (Ithaca: Cornell University Press, 1979), 242; Grodzins, "Phillips," 90–91. The term and the concept of "rule of law" in the Anglo-American context come from the work of the English jurist A. V. Dicey in his *Introduction to the Study of Law of the Constitution* (London: Macmillan, 1885), 171–72, shortly after Phillips died. For Dicey, rule of law meant that the law had one paramount source—the central government—and was itself the supreme source of authority. Phillips used the term once, near the end of his life, referring to tsarist Russia as not obeying "the sober rule of law," a rather different usage than that with which modern jurists are familiar. Phillips, *The Scholar in a Republic* (Boston: Lee and Shepard, 1894), 30.

5. Robert Sauté, *For the Poor and Disenfranchised: Origins of Public Interest Law in the Progressive Era* (New Orleans: Quid Pro, 2014), 3; Stuart A. Scheingold and Austin Sarat, *Something to Believe In: Politics, Professionalism and Cause Lawyering* (Stanford: Stanford University Press, 2004), 24, 31; Nan Aron, *Liberty and Justice for All: Public Interest Law in the 1980s and Beyond* (Boulder: Westview, 1989), 6–8; Robert L. Rabin, "Lawyers for Social Change: Perspectives on Public Interest Law," *Stanford Law Review* 28 (1988): 207–61; Luca Falciola, *Up Against the Law: Radical Lawyers and Social Movements, 1960s–1970s* (Chapel Hill: University of North Carolina Press, 2022).

6. Phillips, *Scholar in a Republic*, 22; Paul Sabin, *Public Citizens: The Attack on Big Government and the Remaking of American Liberalism* (New York: Norton, 2021), 75, 82; "Ralph Nader Urges Harvard Law Students to Pursue Public Service," *Harvard Crimson*, October 10, 2019, https://www.thecrimson.com/article/2019/10/10/nader-hls-talk/, accessed 8/14/23. For Nader in his own words, see *Crashing the Party: Taking on the Corporate Government in an Age of Surrender* (New York: St. Martin's, 2007). On public interest lawyering today, see, for example, Deborah L. Rhode, "Public Interest Law: The Movement at Midlife," *Stanford Law Review* 60 (2008): 2027–84; Louise G. Trubek, "Public Interest Law: Facing the Problems of Maturity," *University of Arkansas at Little Rock Law Review* 33 (2011): 404, 420; Ann Southworth, "What Is Public Interest Law?" *DePaul Law Review* 32 (2013): 493–518. On abolishing homelessness, see Florence Wagman Roisman, "The Lawyer as Abolitionist: Ending Homelessness and Poverty in Our Time," *Saint Louis University Public Law Review* 19 (2000): 238–40.

7. See, for example, Eli Salamon-Abrams, "Remaking Public Defense in an Abolitionist Framework," *Fordham Urban Law Journal* 49 (2022): 436–73; Richard Stacey, "Democratic Jurisprudence and Judicial Review," *Oxford Journal of Legal Studies* 30 (2010): 749–73.

8. Daniel T. Rodgers, *Contested Truths: Keywords in American Politics Since Independence* (New York: Basic Books, 1987), 72, 75; Morton J. Horwitz, *The Transformation of American Law, 1780–1860* (Cambridge, MA: Harvard University Press, 1977), 101–8.

9. Sarah Austin, Preface to *The Province of Jurisprudence Determined*, by John Austin (1832; 2nd ed., London: John Murray, 1861), part 1: xv; Austin, *Province*, lxiv; 5, 8, 10, 15, 120–21; Stephen M. Feldman, "From Premodern to Modern American Jurisprudence: The Onset of Positivism," *Vanderbilt Law Review* 50 (1997): 1387–1405, 1413; W. L. Morison, *John Austin* (Stanford University Pres, 1982), 170–71; Anthony J. Sebok, *Legal Positivism in American Jurisprudence* (Cambridge: Cambridge University Press, 1998), 49–57.

10. Phillips, "The War, Its Cause and Cure," speech at Cooper Institute, *New York Times*, December 20, 1861, p. 8. The classic text on legal positivism in antebellum America is Robert M. Cover, *Justice Accused* (New Haven: Yale University Press, 1975). On positivism today, see Robert P. George, ed., *The Autonomy of Law: Essays on Legal Positivism* (Oxford: Oxford University Press, 1996).

11. W. Caleb McDaniel, *The Problem of Democracy in the Age of Slavery: Garrisonian Abolitionists and Transatlantic Reform* (Baton Rouge: Louisiana State University Press, 2013), 91.

12. Phillips, *The Scholar in a Republic*, 22.

13. Wendell Phillips, *Lectures and Letters*, 2nd ser. (Boston: Lee and Shepard, 1891), iii, iv; Robert D. Marcus, "Wendell Phillips and American Institutions," *Journal of American History* 56 (1969): 43.

14. The *National Anti-Slavery Standard*, founded in New York City by Lydia Maria Child and her husband, David Lee Child, was with the *Liberator* the voice of the American Anti-Slavery Society. Appearing from June 11, 1840, through April 16, 1870, it obviously did not cease publication with the ratification of the Thirteenth Amendment (unlike *The Liberator*) but continued until the ratification of the Fifteenth Amendment. Its editorial policy included advocacy of voting rights for Blacks and women. From 1865 to 1870, its editor was Aaron M. Powell, a Pennsylvania Quaker, abolitionist, and temperance reformer. Not by accident, these were also Phillips's interests.

15. Bartlett, "Wendell Phillips and the Eloquence of Abuse," 509–20.

16. Many general accounts of antislavery celebrate Garrison but more or less slight Phillips, for example, Kate Masur, *Until Justice Be Done: The First Civil Rights Movement from the Revolution to Reconstruction* (New York: Norton, 2021), cites the "radical abolitionists who followed the famous leader William Lloyd Garrison" (xiv), but does not mention of Phillips; Richard S. Newman, *Abolitionism, A Very Short Introduction* (New York: Oxford University Press, 2018), no mention of Phillips; Newman, *The Transformation of American Abolitionism: Fighting Slavery in the Early Republic* (Chapel Hill: University of North Carolina Press, 2022), 178, one passing mention. Two exceptions: Stanley Harrold, *American Abolitionism: Its Direct Political Impact from Colonial Times into Reconstruction* (Charlottesville: University of Virginia Press, 2019), focusing on Phillips and the 1864 presidential campaign; and James Brewer Stewart, *Holy*

Warriors: The Abolitionists and American Slavery, rev. ed. (New York: Hill and Wang, 1996). The latter is an exception, because Stewart has written the leading biography of Phillips. Others that focus on Phillips: Marcus, "Phillips," 50; Louis Filler, introduction to *Wendell Phillips on Civil Rights and Freedom* (New York: Hill and Wang, 1965), xvi–xvii; Roy E. Finkenbine, "Wendell Phillips and 'The Negro's Claim,'" *Massachusetts Historical Review* 7 (2005): 105–19; Lawrence J. Friedman, *Gregarious Saints: Self and Community in American Abolitionism, 1830–1870* (Cambridge: Cambridge University Press, 1982), 45–47; Kenyon Gradert, "Swept into Puritanism: Emerson, Wendell Phillips, and the Roots of Radicalism," *New England Quarterly* 90 (2017): 103–29; Richard Hofstadter, "Wendell Phillips, The Patrician as Agitator," in *The American Political Tradition and the Men Who Made It* (New York: Knopf, 1948), 137–63; Timothy Messet-Kruse, "Eight Hours, Greenbacks, and 'Chinamen': Wendell Phillips, Ira Steward, and the Fate of Labor Reform in Massachusetts," *Labor History* 42 (2001): 133–58; Vernon Louis Parrington, *The Beginnings of Critical Realism*, vol. 3 of *Main Currents in American Thought* (1927; New York: Routledge, 2017), 140–43; the publications in the comprehensive notes of Yacovone's "Race, Radicalism, and Remembering Wendell Phillips," in Aiséirithe and Yacovone, *Phillips*, 327–30; and the major biographies of Phillips: George Lowell Austin, *The Life and Times of Wendell Phillips* (Boston: Lee and Shepard, 1893); James Brewer Stewart, *Wendell Phillips: Liberty's Hero* (Baton Rouge: Louisiana State University Press, 1986), Irving H. Bartlett, *Wendell Phillips, Brahmin Radical* (Boston: Beacon, 1961); and Oscar Sherwin, *Prophet of Liberty: The Life and Times of Wendell Phillips* (New York: Bookman, 1958).

1. ABOLITIONIST

1. Richard Buel Jr., *America on the Brink: How the Political Struggle over the War of 1812 Almost Destroyed the Young Republic* (New York: Macmillan, 2005), 23–24. In the end, the convention debates and resolves did not mention secession. On the impact of the Embargo Act, its enforcement, and the War of 1812 on New England, see Donald R. Hickey, *The War of 1812, A Forgotten Conflict* (Urbana: University of Illinois Press, 2012), 273–74.

2. Austin, *Wendell Phillips*, 18–22; Stewart, *Phillips*, 3–4, 36; Bartlett, *Wendell Phillips*, 1–25; Sherwin, *Phillips*, 1–32.

3. Stewart, *Phillips*, 6, 7, 12; Austin, *Phillips*, 26–27. The subject of the individual motivations of reformers in antebellum American is one that intrigues historians. See, for example, Steven Mintz, *Moralists and Modernizers: America's Pre–Civil War Reformers* (Baltimore: Johns Hopkins University Press, 1995), xvi–xvii. Frank J. Sulloway's much cited and highly controversial thesis is that later-born

sons are more likely to rebel than their older brothers, because the older sons have taken up the higher-status roles that the family offered. His focus was on younger sons in Revolutionary times, but the abolitionist era may be likened to the earlier period. See Sulloway, *Born to Rebel: Birth Order, Family Dynamics, and Creative Lives* (New York: Pantheon, 1996), xviii and after.

4. Quoted in Austin, *Phillips*, 32.

5. Carl Bode, *The American Lyceum: Town Meeting of the Mind* (Carbondale: Southern Illinois University Press, 1968), 50; Peter Charles Hoffer, *Daniel Webster and the Unfinished Constitution* (Lawrence: University Press of Kansas, 2021), 14. On oratory in the early antebellum period, see, for example, Kimberly K. Smith, *The Dominion of Voice: Riot, Reason, and Romance in Antebellum Politics* (Lawrence: University Press of Kansas, 1999); and James Perrin Warren, *Culture of Eloquence: Oratory and Reform in Antebellum America* (State College: Pennsylvania State University Press, 2010).

6. Boston as the Athens of America: Thomas H. O'Connor, *The Athens of America, Boston, 1825–1845* (Amherst: University of Massachusetts Press, 2006). Though Phillips was never a Jacksonian, the influence of Jacksonian individualistic reform reached out beyond politics. See Marvin Meyers, *The Jacksonian Persuasion: Politics and Belief* (Palo Alto: Stanford University Press, 1957), 207.

7. Austin, *Phillips*, 35, 39; Stewart, *Phillips*, 28, 29. Stewart suggests that these historical figures were substitutes for Wendell's father. Certainly they were all father figures.

8. Wendell Phillips to Frederick Douglass, 1845, in the preface to Douglass's *Narrative of the Life of Frederick Douglass, An American Slave* (Boston: Anti-Slavery Office, 1845), xiii, xiv. In the coming years, Phillips and Douglass would come to distrust one another, and even, on Phillips's side, publicly accuse one another of betrayal. The question then and later was whether white men should take the lead in fostering racial equality. Stephen Kantorwitz, *More Than Freedom: Fighting for Black Citizenship in a White Republic, 1829–1889* (New York: Penguin, 2012), 151–53.

At the time, the term "adolescence" meant growing into maturity. As a stage in the development of personal Identity, it was not explored until the early twentieth century. But it is not clear that Phillips experienced the "new birth" of his faculties, understanding, and empathy that accompany adolescence. G. Stanley Hall, *Adolescence* (New York: Appleton, 1904), xiii. Phillips had no identity crisis, no challenge to parental or conventional values, no rebellion. Thus he had no strong sense of personal identity apart from class and clade. Erik H. Erikson, *Identity: Youth and Crisis* (New York: Norton, 1968), 128–35.

9. Wendell Phillips, "Welcome to George Thompson," November 26, 1850, *Speeches and Letters*, 2nd ser., 27; Louis D. Brandeis, "The Harvard Law School," *Green Bag* 2d 11 (1904): 490–92; Michael von der Linn, "Harvard Law School's

Promotional Literature," *Green Bag* 2d 13 (1906): 432–38; Cover, *Justice Accused,* 243; R. Kent Newmyer, *Supreme Court Justice Joseph Story, Statesman of the Old Republic* (Chapel Hill: University of North Carolina Press, 2004), 173; Arthur E. Sunderland, *The Law at Harvard: A History of Ideas and Men, 1817–1967* (Cambridge, MA: Harvard University Press, 1967), 92–149.

10. M. H. Hoeflich, "John Austin and Joseph Story: Two Nineteenth-Century Perspectives on the Utility of the Civil Law for the Common Lawyer," *American Journal of Legal History* 29 (1985): 36–77, traces certain parallels in the two men's use of Roman law, but does not show that either was aware of the other. Story had access to almost all of the major European treatises through gifts to the Harvard Law School and the Boston Athenaeum, but Austin's lectures were published only after his death in 1859. Thus Austin was absent from Story, *Commentaries on the Constitutions of the United States* (Boston: Hilliard, Gray, 1833); *Commentary on the Conflict of Laws* (Boston: Hilliard, Gray, 1834); and *Commentaries on Equity Jurisprudence* (Boston: Little, Brown, 1836). Nor does Austin appear in the William Wetmore edition of Story's *Letters* (London: J. Chapman, 1851). But see Cover, *Justice Accused,* 119, 131–48; Phillips, "Joseph Story," *Liberator,* September 11, 1846; *United States v.* Amistad 40 U. S. 518 (1841), finding that slaves taken from Africa to Cuba in violation of a treaty with Spain were free and could use violent force to secure that freedom; *Prigg v. Pennsylvania* 41 U. S. 539 (1842), finding that a Pennsylvania antikidnaping law violated the Fugitive Slave Act of 1793 and the state could not proceed against Prigg for recapturing a runaway slave.

11. Austin, *Phillips,* 43–44.

12. *Directory of the City of Boston* (Boston: George Adams, 1850), 262; *Boston Directory* (Boston: George Adams, 1851), 198; (1855), 240; (1856) 269; (1861), 354; Grodzins, "Phillips," 106; *Albany Law Journal* 5 (1872): 17, 33.

13. On Lowell and textiles, Thomas Dublin, *Women at Work: The Transformation of Work and Community in Lowell Massachusetts, 1826–1860* (New York: Columbia University Press, 1979), 14–22; on contract and labor law, Hoffer, *Litigation Nation: A Cultural History of Lawsuits in America* (Lanham, MD: Rowman and Littlefield, 2019), 81–106; on Francis Cabot Lowell, Chaim M. Rosenberg, *The Life and Times of Francis Cabot Lowell, 1775–1817* (Lanham, MD: Lexington, 2011), 273–320.

14. Phillips, "The Boston Mob," October 21, 1855, Pease, *Speeches,* 2nd ser., 213. Often described as Garrison's ally, his friend, his right arm, his spokesman, Phillips was all of these, but Garrison spoke with religious and moral fervor. Phillips, I argue here, was still a lawyer and spoke as a lawyer.

15. Phillips, *Eulogy of Garrison: Remarks of Wendell Phillips at the Funeral of William Lloyd Garrison* (Boston: Lee and Shepard, 1884), 10; Bertram Wyatt-Brown, "Proslavery and Anti-slavery Intellectuals," in *Antislavery Reconsidered: New Perspectives on the Abolitionists,* ed. Lewis Perry and Michael Fellman (Ba-

ton Rouge: Louisiana State University Press, 1979), 317, 319; Manisha Sinha, *The Slave's Cause: A History of Abolition* (New Haven: Yale University Press, 2012), 264–65; Stewart, *Phillips,* 44.

16. Stewart, *Phillips,* 40–41; Austin, *Phillips,* 44.

17. Samuel Sewall, *The Selling of Joseph: A Memorial* (Boston: Greene and Allen, 1700), 1; Wendy Warren, *New England Bound: Slavery and Colonization in Early America* (New York: Norton, 2016), 221–22; "Petition of Prince Hall and others, January 13, 1777, To the Honorable Counsel & House of [Representa]tives of the State of Massachusetts Bay in General Court assembled," *Collections of the Massachusetts Historical Society,* 5th ser., 3 (1877): 436–37; *Commonwealth v. Nathaniel Jennison,* Massachusetts 1783, unreported (Cushing, C. J.).

18. Northwest Ordinance of 1787, https://www.archives.gov/milestone-documents/northwest-ordinance, accessed 7/6/23; on Jefferson and the ordinance, Peter S. Onuf, *Statehood and Union: A History of the Northwest Ordinance* (Notre Dame, IN: University of Notre Dame Press, 2019). On emancipation in the North, Arthur Zilversmit, *The First Emancipation: The Abolition of Slavery in the North* (Chicago: University of Chicago Press, 1967). On manumission in the Upper South, Lacy K. Ford, Jr., *Deliver Us from Evil: The Slavery Question in the Old South* (New York: Oxford University Press, 2009), 19–48.

19. "Yield nothing," quoted in Robert Pierce Forbes, *The Missouri Compromise and Its Aftermath: Slavery and the Meaning of America,* 3rd ed. (Chapel Hill: University of North Carolina Press, 2007), 93; "a wolf by the ear": Thomas Jefferson to John Holmes, April 22, 1820, Thomas Jefferson Papers, special collections, University of Virginia Library.

20. William Lee Miller, *Arguing About Slavery: John Quincy Adams and the Great Battle in the United States Congress* (New York: Knopf, 1996), 29. On resistance to abolitionist literature in the Deep South, Ford, *Deliver Us from Evil,* 449–80. See, generally, Richard S. Newman, *The Transformation of American Abolitionism: Fighting Slavery in the Early Republic* (Chapel Hill: University of North Carolina Press, 2002), 131–75.

21. The literature on the origins of the immediate abolitionist movement in Massachusetts is immense. On the origins of the *Liberator,* see McDaniel, *The Problem of Democracy,* 38; and Richard S. Newman, *The Transformation of American Abolitionism: Fighting Slavery in the Early Republic* (Chapel Hill: University of North Carolina Press, 2002), 114.

22. On Garrison, John L. Thomas, *Liberator: William Lloyd Garrison, A Biography* (Boston: Little, Brown, 1963), is the industry standard, but see also Aileen S. Kraditor, *Means and Ends in American Abolitionism: Garrison and His Critics on Strategy and Tactics, 1834–1850* (New York: Pantheon, 1969); Louis S. Gerteis, *Morality and Utility in American Antislavery Reform* (Chapel Hill: University of North Carolina Press, 1987); and Merton L. Dillon, *The Abolitionists: The Growth*

of a Dissenting Minority (DeKalb: University of Northern Illinois Press, 1974), all of which note that Garrison's was not the only voice in the movement.

23. Brewer, "Wendell Phillips Is the Subtlest, Stubbornest Fact of the Times," in Aiséirithe and Yacovone, *Phillips,* 34–35.

24. Wendell Phillips, "Resolution Presented to the Massachusetts Anti-slavery Society," Lynn, Massachusetts, March 28, 1837, in *Speeches, Lectures and Letters of Wendell Phillips,* ed. Theodore C. Pease, 2nd ser. (Boston: Lee and Shepard, 1891), 1 (hereafter Pease, ed., *Speeches,* 2nd ser.).

25. On the Alien and Sedition Acts controversy, see Hoffer, *The Free Press Crisis of 1800: Thomas Cooper's Trial for Seditious Libel* (Lawrence: University Press of Kansas, 2011), 89–129; on the gag rule, see Hoffer, *John Quincy Adams and the Gag Rule, 1835–1850* (Lawrence: University Press of Kansas, 2017), 6–28.

26. Henry Mayer, *All on Fire: William Lloyd Garrison and the Abolition of Slavery* (New York: St. Martins, 1998), 110–11; Newman, *American Abolitionism,* 131, 133.

27. Owen W. Muelder, *Theodore Dwight Weld and the American Anti-Slavery Society* (Jefferson, NC: McFarland, 2011), 38–39.

28. "Wendell Phillips on the Election," *New York Times,* November 9, 1860, p. 8; Stewart, *Phillips,* 56. Phillips had obviously read the Adams diary, but volume 3, to which his speech referred, was not published until the 1870s, edited by his son, Charles Francis Adams (himself an antislavery congressman).

29. This and subsequent paragraphs taken from Hoffer, *John Quincy Adams and the Gag Rule,* 15–27.

30. Miller, *Arguing about Slavery,* 140–49.

31. William Slade, speech in the House of Representatives, December 16, 1835, 24th Cong., 1st sess., 13 Register of Debates in Congress 1, 1962 (hereafter Reg. Deb.); and Hammond motion, December 18, 1835, 24th Cong., 1st sess., 13 Reg. Deb. 1, 1966. http://memory.loc.gov/cgi-bin/ampage?collId=llrd&fileName=026/llrd026.db&recNum=0>, accessed 7/10/23.

32. James Henry Hammond, speech in the House, February 1, 1836, 24th Cong., 2nd sess., 13 Reg. Deb. 2, 2448–62, http://memory.loc.gov/cgi-bin/ampage?collId=llrd&fileName=027/llrd027.db&recNum=31, accessed 7/10/23.

33. Pinckney committee resolution, May 26, 1836, 24th Cong. 1st sess., 13 Reg. Deb. 2, 4028, http://memory.loc.gov/cgi-bin/ampage?collId=llrd&fileName=027/llrd027.db&recNum=31, accessed 7/10/23.

34. Daniel Wirls, "'The Only Method of Avoiding Everlasting Debate': The Overlooked Senate Gag Rule for Antislavery Petitions," *Journal of the Early Republic* 27 (2007): 115–38; James M. McPherson, "The Fight Against the Gag Rule: Joshua Leavitt and Antislavery Insurgency in the Whig Party, 1839–1842," *Journal of Negro History* 48 (1963): 177–95.

35. Kenneth I. Kersh, *Free Speech: Rights and Privileges Under the Law* (Santa Barbara, CA: ABC-CLIO, 2003), 81; Thomas Hart Benton quoted in Michael

Kent Curtis, *"The People's Darling Privilege": Struggles for Freedom of Expression in American History* (Durham, NC: Duke University Press, 2000), 141; executive board of the AASS quoted in Sinha, *The Slave's Cause,* 250.

36. Adams quoted in James Oakes, *The Scorpion's Sting: Antislavery and the Coming of the Civil War* (New York: Norton, 2014), 137; Robert Remini, *John Quincy Adams* (New York: Times Books, 2002), 139–40 (Adams "despises" radical abolitionism); Leonard L. Richards, *The Life and Times of Congressman John Quincy Adams* (New York: Oxford University Press, 1988), 113ff. (Adams was motivated in part by political spite); David F. Ericson, "John Quincy Adams: Apostle of Union," in *Blackwell Companion to John Adams and John Quincy Adams,* ed. David Waldstreicher (New York: Wiley, 2013), 375–76 (evolution of his views from tolerating slavery to absolute opposition); Matthew Mason, "John Quincy Adams and the Tangled Politics of Slavery," in *Blackwell Companion,* 402–21 (the impact of politics on Adams); Jonathan Bryant, *Dark Places of the Earth: The Voyage of the Slave Ship* Antelope (New York: Norton, 2015), 178 (on the *Antelope*).

37. Adams, diary entry, December 26, 1835, *Memoirs of John Quincy Adams,* ed. Charles Francis Adams (Philadelphia: Lippincott, 1874), 9:268.

38. Adams, diary entry, January 12, 1836, *Memoirs,* 9:271.

39. Adams, diary entry, May 26, 1836, *Memoirs,* 9:287.

40. May 26, 1836, 24th Cong. 1st sess., 13 Reg. Deb. 1, 4058, 4060; Adams, diary entry, May 26, 1836, *Memoirs,* 9: 287, 288; Walter S. Franklin to James K. Polk, February 1836, *Correspondence of James K. Polk,* ed. Herbert Weaver (Nashville: Vanderbilt University Press, 1975), 3:663.

41. Adams, speech in the House, December 26, 1836, 24th Cong. 2nd sess., 13 Reg. Deb. 1, 1156–57, http://memory.loc.gov/cgi-bin/ampage?collId=llrd&fileName=027/llrd027.db&recNum=31, accessed 7/10/23.

42. Richard P. McCormick, *The Second Party System: Party Formation in the Jacksonian Era* (New York: Norton, 1966) 14–16 (purpose of parties was to win presidency).

43. Phillips, Address to the Anti-Slavery Society of Lynn, March 28, 1837, in Pease, ed., *Speeches,* 2nd ser., 1, 2, 5.

44. Phillips quoted in Merton L. Dillon, *Elijah P. Lovejoy, Abolitionist Editor* (Urbana: University of Illinois Press, 1961), 194; Paul Simon, *Elijah Lovejoy, Freedom's Champion* (Carbondale: University of Southern Illinois Press, 1994), 154–62, 185, 192.

45. The meeting is depicted in Bartlett, *Phillips,* 48–49.

46. Phillips, "Murder of Lovejoy," December 8, 1837, in *Speeches, Lectures, and Letters of Wendell Phillips,* ed. James Redpath (Boston: Lee and Shepard, 1884) (hereafter *Speeches,* 1st ser., 1884), 2, 4, 6, 7, 8.

47. Alvan Stewart, "Response to the Message of Governor [William L.] Marcy," September 1836, in *Writings and Speeches of Alvan Stewart on Slavery,* ed. Luther

Rawson Marsh (New York: Burdick, 1860), 74; Frederick J. Blue, *No Taint of Compromise: Crusaders in Anti-Slavery Politics* (Baton Rouge: Louisiana State University Press, 2006), 15–36; Corey M. Brooks, *Liberty Power: Anti-Slavery Third Parties and the Transformation of American Politics* (Chicago: University of Chicago Press, 2020), 32; Wiecek, *Anti-Slavery Constitutionalism in America*, 249; Ernst, "Legal Positivism," 345.

48. "Lyceums," in *The Early Republic and Antebellum America: An Encyclopedia of Social, Political, Cultural, and Economic History*, ed. Christopher G. Bates (New York: Routledge, 2015), 2:593–94.

2. AGITATOR

1. The difficulties of launching the Liberty Party, and the key role of Birney in it, are the subjects of D. Laurence Rogers, *Apostles of Equality: The Birneys, the Republicans, and the Civil War* (Lansing: Michigan State University Press, 2011), 119 and after.

2. The complexity of British emancipation in the Victorian period is traced in Richard Huzzey, *Freedom Burning: Anti-Slavery and Empire in Victorian Britain* (Ithaca, NY: Cornell University Press, 2009), 5–13. On the end of the slave trade, see Christopher Brown, *Moral Capital: Foundations of British Abolitionism* (Chapel Hill: University of North Carolina Press, 2006); and J. R. Kerr-Ritchie, *Rites of August First: Emancipation Day in the Black Atlantic World* (Baton Rouge: University of Louisiana Press, 2007).

3. *National Anti-Slavery Standard*, August 13, 1840, p. 1; Huzzey, *Freedom Burning*, 14–15.

4. Alice Felt Tyler, *Freedom's Ferment: Phases of American Social History to 1860* (1944; repr., Case Press, 2007); Phillips, "Cotton, the Corner Stone of Slavery," address to the British India Society, July 6, 1840, in *Speeches, Second Series*, 13, 14, 15, 18; Sven Beckert, *Empire of Cotton: A Global History* (New York: Random House, 2014), 98–118.

5. James Henry Hammond, *Speech in the Senate, March 4, 1858, On the Admission of Kansas* (Washington, DC: Lemuel Towers, 1858), 9–10.

6. Steve Luxenberg, "The Jim Crow Car," *Washington Post*, February 20, 2019, https://www.washingtonpost.com/news/magazine/wp/2019/02/20/feature/the-forgotten-northern-pre-civil-war-origins-of-jim-crow/, accessed 8/18/23; *Liberator*, 12, no. 7, February 18, 1842, p. 26; Louis Ruchames, "Jim Crow Railroads in Massachusetts," *American Quarterly* 8 (156): 61–75. Bartlett recognizes that this was "a lawyer's brief, clear cut, well-reasoned, with cases cited to support" his contentions. Bartlett, *Phillips*, 87.

7. Phillips, "Remarks on the Opinion of the City Solicitor," *Report of the Minority of the City School Board* (Boston: A. J. Wright, 1846), 28, 29, 30, 33, 34;

Robert J. Cottrol, Raymond T. Diamond, and Leland B. Ware, *Brown v. Board of Education: Caste, Culture, and the Constitution* (Lawrence: University Press of Kansas, 2003), 15–18; *Roberts v. City of Boston* 59 Mass. 198 (1850); Edward Stanwood, "Memoir of Peleg Whitman Chandler," *Proceedings of the Massachusetts Historical Society* (Boston: MHS, 1907), 287.

8. Phillips, "Remarks" 34; Bartlett, *Phillips*, 89–90.

9. *National Anti-Slavery Standard*, February 17, 1842; *Liberator*, 12, no. 10, March 11, 1842; Bartlett, *Phillips*, 116.

10. *Liberator*, 12, no. 45, November 11, 1842; Wiecek, *Sources*, 237.

11. Phillips, *The Constitution a Pro-Slavery Compact, with extracts from the Madison Papers* (New York: American Anti-Slavery Society, 1844), 4, 5; Phillips, *Can Abolitionists Vote or Take Office Under the United States Constitution?* (New York: American Anti-Slavery Society, 1844), 10, 11.

12. Phillips, *Constitution,* 5, 6; Randy E. Barnett, "The Significance of Lysander Spooner" (January 4, 2016), Liberty Matters, https://oll.libertyfund.org/page/liberty-matters-randy-barnett-lysander-spooner#lm-spooner, accessed 8/18/23.

13. U. S. Const. art. I, § 2, cl. 3; art. 4, § 2, cl. 3; art. I, § 9. Whether the Constitution was proslavery is still a matter of controversy. Yes: David Waldstreicher, *Slavery's Constitution: From Revolution to Ratification* (New York: Hill and Wang, 2010). No: Sean Wilentz, *No Property in Man: Slavery and Anti-Slavery at the Nation's Founding* (Cambridge, MA: Harvard University Press, 2019).

14. Bartlett, *Phillips*, 82, 127; Phillips, *Review of Lysander Spooner's Essay on the Unconstitutionality of Slavery . . .* (Boston: Andrews and Prentice, 1847), 5–6, 26. The modern doctrine of strict adherence to original texts of the law is called originalism or original intent. *Black's Law Dictionary*, 6th. ed. (St. Paul: West, 1991), p. 1133. The literature on originalism is explored in Jack M. Balkin, *Living Originalism* (Cambridge, MA: Harvard University Press, 2011). Balkin's work was reviewed by Lawrence Solum, an expert on originalism, in "Construction and Constraint," *Jerusalem Review of Legal Studies* 7 (2013): 17–34. In a sophisticated linguistic essay, Solum sees originalism as a family of theories, though the term "clade" might be more appropriate, all of which concern (but none settle) the vexing question of constraining the discretion of judges. A more orthodox exposition of that jurisprudence is Antonin Scalia, *The Essential Scalia* (New York: Crown, 2020), 15 and after.

15. Eric Foner, *Free Soil, Free Labor, Free Men: The Ideology of the Republican Party before the Civil War* (New York: Oxford University Press, 1970), 12–13.

16. Joel H. Silbey, *Storm Over Texas: The Annexation Crisis and the Road to Civil War* (New York: Oxford University Press, 2005), 28–91.

17. Charles G. Sellers, *James K. Polk, Continentalist, 1843–1846* (Princeton: Princeton University Press, 1966), 108–61.

18. Corey M. Brooks, *Liberty Power: Antislavery Parties and the Transformation of American Politics* (Chicago: University of Chicago Press, 2020), 42, 63; Foner, *Free Soil*, 127.

19. William W. Freehling, *The Road to Disunion: Secessionists at Bay, 1776–1854* (New York Oxford University Press, 1991), 458–63. On the war, Peter Guardino, *The Dead March: A History of the Mexican-American War* (Cambridge, MA: Harvard University Press, 2017). The classic work is Justin Harvey Smith, *The War with Mexico*, 2 vols. (New York: Macmillan, 1919).

20. Helen J. Knowles-Gardner, "Learning the Law in 1830s Massachusetts: The Contrasting Experiences of Wendell Phillips and Lysander Spooner," February 11, 2021, 28, http://dx.doi.org/10.2139/ssrn.3760209, accessed 8/18/23; Stewart, *Phillips*, 123; Spooner quoted in Arthur Zilversmit, "Was Slavery Unconstitutional before the Thirteenth Amendment? Lysander Spooner's Theory of Interpretation," in *Abolitionism and American Law*, ed. John V. McKivigan (New York: Routledge, 1999), 66–67 (Spooner was later known as a leading anarchist); Steve J. Shone, *Lysander Spooner, American Anarchist* (Lanham, MD: Rowman and Littlefield, 2010).

21. Lysander Spooner, *The Unconstitutionality of Slavery* (Boston: Bela Marsh, 1845), 17, 18, 22, 45, 61, 65, 67–68, 154–55.

22. Wendell Phillips, *Review of Lysander Spooner's Essay on the Unconstitutionality of Slavery* . . . (Boston: Andrews and Prentice, 1847), 3.

23. Phillips, *Review of Spooner*, 4.

24. Phillips, *Review of Spooner*, 5. The fiery trial is a reference to Eric Foner, *The Fiery Trial: Abraham Lincoln and American Slavery* (New York: Norton, 2010).

25. Phillips, *Review of Spooner*, 7, 8. When in 1858 Spooner asked Phillips's advice about circulating an antislavery handbill in the South, Phillips was kind, but thought the idea unworkable. When Spooner floated a plan to kidnap Governor John Wise of Virginia, Phillips demurred, and the idea fizzled out. Bartlett, *Phillips*, 210, 212. No mention of Phillips's review of Spooner ten years earlier appears in Bartlett. Stewart, *Phillips*, does not mention the 108-page essay. Nor does Sherwin, *Phillips*.

26. Phillips, *Review of Spooner*, 8. I cannot find where Phillips read Austin. *The Province of Justice Determined* was published in England in 1832, but Austin was not cited in any of Joseph Story's commentaries. Austin's work did not become popular until after he died in 1859. Again, Phillips's departure from natural-law principles marked him as a modern rather than a premodern jurisprudent. Stephen Matthew Feldman, "From Premodern to Modern Jurisprudence: The Onset of Positivism," *Vanderbilt Law Review* 50, no. 6 (1997): 1394–95.

27. H. L. A. Hart, "Bentham On Sovereignty," *Irish Jurist* 2nd ser., 2 (1967): 327, 328.

28. See, for example, Robert Cover, *Justice Accused* (New Haven: Yale University Press, 1975), 119 and after. It is, however, the position of other law teachers today, for example, Ronald Dworkin, that judges did have the jurisprudential means to strike down the Fugitive Slave Act. See Dworkin, *Law's Empire* (Cambridge: Harvard University Press, 1976), 441.

29. Phillips, *Review of Spooner*, 12, 13, 15. Actually, Spooner had a point: because of the federal system embodied in the Judiciary Act of 1789, federal courts sitting in a state followed that state's law in matters not relating to federal statutes. Hence what was law in the federal district court of Maine might not—indeed in certain questions of domestic relations was not—law in the federal district court of Mississippi. Neither man explored this point, however.

30. Joseph Story, *Commentaries on Equity Jurisprudence* (Boston: Hilliard, Gray, 1836), 1:14 states that equity operates only where law does not give relief; it does not contradict law, but only expands it. Phillips, *Review of Spooner*, 21, 22.

31. Phillips, *Review of Spooner*, 28, 29, 33. But the problem of fictive consent is one that continues to interest legal scholars and political scientists. See, for example, Randy Barnett, *Restoring the Lost Constitution* (Princeton: Princeton University Press, 2004), 29 and after, a book that won the Lysander Spooner Award for "advancing the literature of liberty."

32. "The Slave Med," aka *Commonwealth v. Aves*, 35 Mass. 193 (1836) (Shaw, C.J.).

33. Phillips, *Review of Spooner*, 93; Stewart, *Phillips*, 133–34; Cover, *Justice Accused*, 156–57.

34. Phillips, *The Philosophy of the Abolition Movement* (1853), 23, 24.

35. Spooner, *Unconstitutionality of Slavery, Part Second* (Boston: Bela Marsh, 1847), 234, 276; Spooner, *A Defense for Fugitive Slaves* (Boston: Bela Marsh, 1850), 5, 19, 23, 24. Neither book cites Austin.

36. Phillips, "Right of Petition," March 28, 1837, in Pease, ed., *Speeches*, 2nd ser., 5.

37. Phillips to Frederick Douglass, *Narrative*, xv; Stewart, *Phillips*, 127–30.

38. On popular constitutionalism, see Akhil Amar, *America's Unwritten Constitution* (New York: Basic Books, 2011) and Christian Fritz, *American Sovereigns: The People and America's Constitutional Tradition before the Civil War* (New York: Cambridge University Press, 2007); on Phillips and popular constitutionalism, see Michael Les Benedict, "Wendell Phillips, the Constitution, and Constitutional Politics before the Civil War," in Aiséirithe and Yacovone, eds., *Phillips*, 138.

39. Bartlett, *Phillips*, 106–9; Howard N. Mayer, ed., *The Magnificent Activist: Thomas Wentworth Higginson* (New York: Da Capo, 2000), 65. Higginson, *Wendell Phillips* (Boston: Lee and Shepard, 1884), vii.

3. RADICAL

1. See, for example, Phillips to Ralph Waldo Emerson, July 22, 1851, in Irving Bartlett, "The Philosopher and the Activist: New Letters from Emerson to Wendell Phillips," *New England Quarterly* 62 (1989): 286; Richard H. Leach, "Benjamin Robbins Curtis, Judicial Misfit," *New England Quarterly* 26 (1952): 518; but see James Brewer Stewart, *Abolitionist Politics and the Coming of the Civil War*

(Amherst: University of Massachusetts Press, 2008), 5, 6, 26: "Clearly, Phillips spoke the feelings of most Massachusetts voters," on at least some occasions.

2. California State Constitution of 1849, https://www.sos.ca.gov/archives/collections/constitutions/1849/, accessed 7/23/23.

3. On the 1850 Clay compromise: Robert Remini, *Henry Clay: Statesman for the Union* (New York: Norton, 1991), 732–37; actually, Clay's contribution to the settlement of the issues in Congress was much more complicated. See the essays in, eds., *A Fire Bell in the Night: The Missouri Crisis at 200*, ed. Jeffrey L. Pasley and John Craig Hammond (Columbia: University of Missouri Press, 2021).

4. On lawyers in the abolitionist movement, William Wiecek, "Latimer: The Problem of Unjust Laws," in *Antislavery Reconsidered*, ed. Perry and Fellman, 232–33; Wiecek, *The Sources of Antislavery Constitutionalism in America, 1760–1848* (Ithaca, NY: Cornell University Press, 1979), 228–75; Daniel R. Ernst, "Legal Positivism, Abolitionist Litigation, and the New Jersey Slave Case of 1845," *Law and History Review* 4 (1986): 337–65; Daniel Farbman, "Resistance Lawyering," *California Law Review* 107 (2019): 1877–1954; Randy E. Barnett, "From Antislavery Lawyer to Chief Justice: The Remarkable Career of Salmon P. Chase," *Case Western Reserve Law Review* 63 (2013): 654–701; Len Gougeon, "1838: Ellis Grey Loring and a Journal for the Times," *Studies in the American Renaissance* (1990): 33–47; Samuel Shapiro, *Richard Henry Dana Jr.* (Lansing: Michigan State University Press, 1961), 34 and after. On Sumner's abolitionism, see Williamjames Hull Hoffer, *The Caning of Charles Sumner: Honor, Idealism, and the Origins of the Civil War* (Baltimore: Johns Hopkins University Press, 2010), 21.

5. Phillips, [Untitled], in *Liberator*, May 30, 1839. On Seward's antislavery stance, see Hoffer, *Seward's Law: Country Lawyering, Relational Rights, and Slavery* (Ithaca, NY: Cornell University Press, 2023), 23–26; 48, 73. By contrast, when nonlawyer abolitionists such as Gerritt Smith tried to make legal arguments, they led nowhere. See, for example, William E. Nelson, "The Impact of the Antislavery Movement upon Styles of Judicial Reasoning in Nineteenth-Century America," *Harvard Law Review* 97 (1974): 513–66.

6. Phillips, "Welcome to Thompson," *Speeches*, 2nd ser., 32; Sherwin, *Prophet*, 370.

7. Phillips, "Welcome to Thompson," 33.

8. "Phillips, "Welcome to Thompson," 33.

9. Fugitive Slave Act of 1850, 9 Stat. at Large (US) 462, 463, § 6 (1850).

10. Phillips, "Welcome to Thompson," 34, 35.

11. Gary Collison, *Shadrach Minkins: From Fugitive Slave to Citizen* (Cambridge, MA: Harvard University Press, 1997), 91–150; Bartlett, *Phillips*, 148–49.

12. Millard Fillmore, Proclamation, February 18, 1851, in *The Papers of Daniel Webster*, ed. Charles M. Wiltse and Michael J. Birkner (Hanover, NH: University Press of New England for Dartmouth College, 1986), 7:206–7.

13. 9 Stat. 462 (1850); Phillips, "Public Opinion," January 28, 1852, *Speeches, Lectures and Letters* (1863), 48.

14. Phillips, "Public Opinion," 33. On Seward and relational rights, see Hoffer, *Seward's Law*, 3–11, 46–49. Seward fully explored the idea of hospitality in his brief in *Jones v. Van Zandt*, 46 U. S. 215 (1847). Whether Phillips had read Seward's brief, published as a pamphlet, or merely thought in the same fashion cannot be determined, but Phillips could not have missed this case or its significance, or Seward's part in it. Frederic Bancroft, *Life of William H. Seward* (New York: Harper Brothers, 1900), 1:180–82.

15. Phillips, "Public Opinion" 34.

16. Phillips, "Public Opinion," 34, 35.

17. Stewart, *Phillips*, 41–42.

18. Daniel Farbman, "Resistance Lawyering," 1877–1927.

19. Stewart, *Phillips*, 46–51, 71–72; Nancy Isenberg, *Sex and Citizenship in Antebellum America* (Chapel Hill: University of North Carolina Press, 1998), xii, xiii, 87; Debra Gold Hansen, "The Boston Female Anti-Slavery Society and the Limits of Gender Politics," in *The Abolitionist Sisterhood: Women's Political Culture in Antebellum America*, ed. Jean Fagin Yellin and John C. Van Horne (Ithaca, NY: Cornell University Press, 1994), 45–66.

20. Elizabeth Cady Stanton, *A History of Woman Suffrage* (Rochester, NY: Fowler and Wells, 1889), 1: 70–71; N. E. H. Hull, *The Woman Who Dared to Vote: The Trial of Susan B. Anthony* (Lawrence: University Press of Kansas, 2012), xvii–xxiii.

21. Phillips, "Resolution on Women's Rights," October 15, 1851, *in Speeches, Lectures, and Letters* (Boston: Redpath, 1863), 11, 12.

22. Phillips, "Resolution," 12.

23. Phillips, "Public Opinion" January 28, 1852, *Speeches and Letters* (Boston: Lee and Shepard, 1863), 35, 36, 52, 46.

24. Once again, in this he anticipated Benjamin Barber's argument in *Strong Democracy*. Both men rejected the "thin" prudential version of liberal politics, "means to exclusively individualistic and private ends." See Barber, *Strong Democracy: Participatory Politics for a New Age* (Berkeley: University of California Press, 2004).

25. Phillips, "The Surrender of Sims," January 30, 1852, *Speeches and Letters*, 62.

26. Phillips, "First Anniversary of the Rendition of Sims," April 12, 1852, *Speeches and Letters*, 95.

27. Phillips, "First Anniversary," 75.

28. Phillips, "First Anniversary," 78.

29. Phillips, "The Philosophy of the Abolitionist Movement," speech in Boston, January 27, 1853; reprinted as Anti-Slavery Tract No. 8, new ser. (New York: Anti-Slavery Society, 1860), 3, 4, 5.

30. Phillips, "Philosophy," 8, 9.

31. Phillips, "Philosophy," 9.

32. Phillips, "Philosophy," 10.

33. Phillips, "Philosophy," 11, 12.

34. Phillips, "Philosophy," 12.

35. Phillips, "Philosophy," 15, 16.

36. Phillips, "Philosophy," 17, 18. William Jay was the son of Chief Justice John Jay, the first chief justice of the US Supreme Court. A learned abolitionist, William Jay was the president of the New York Anti-Slavery Society. His *Inquiry into the Character and Tendency of the American Colonization and Anti-Slavery Societies* (New York: Williams, 1838), 192, found that removal of slavery by colonization was "both morally and physically impossible." The only question was whether immediate emancipation was the only effective answer. William Jay believed that gradual emancipation was both sinful and ineffective as well. It was "so full of difficulty" that even as a political expedient it was unworkable (193).

37. Phillips, "Philosophy," 19.

38. Phillips, "Philosophy," 20.

39. Sims case, 61 Mass. 285, 291, 293 (1851) (Shaw, C. J.); Leonard W. Levy, *The Law of the Commonwealth and Chief Justice Shaw* (Cambridge, MA: Harvard University Press, 1957), 78–83, 88. But that did not mean Phillips ceased to be a lawyer. It merely meant he ceased paying bar dues. That would get him removed from the bar membership and from representing people in court, but he could still advise.

40. Earl Maltz, *Fugitive Slave on Trial: The Anthony Burns Case and Abolitionist Outrage* (Lawrence: University Press of Kansas, 2010), 57 and after; Gordon Barker, *The Imperfect Revolution: Anthony Burns and the Landscape of Race in Antebellum America* (Kent, OH: Kent State University Press, 2010), 3 and after; Paul Finkelman, "Legal Ethics and Fugitive Slaves," *Cardozo Law Review* 17 (1995): 1793–1858.

41. Phillips, "Argument before the Committee on Federal Relations of the Massachusetts Legislature, in Support of the Petitions for the Removal of Edward Greely Loring from the Office of Judge of Probate, February 20, 1855," *Speeches and Letters*, 155, 156.

42. Phillips, "Argument," 164, 165, 170.

43. Phillips, "Boston Mob," *Speeches and Letters*, 217.

44. Kenneth M. Stampp, "The Concept of a Perpetual Union," *Journal of American History* 65 (1978): 5–33. On the Dred Scott case, see *Dred Scott v. Sandford*, 60 U. S. 393 (1857); Don E. Fehrenbacher, *The Dred Scott Case: Its Significance in American Law and Politics* (New York: Oxford University Press, 1978); Paul Finkelman, *Dred Scott v. Sandford: A Brief History with Documents* (New York: Bedford, 1997); Mark A. Graber, *Dred Scott and the Problem of Constitutional Evil* (New York: Cambridge University Press, 2006); and Timothy S. Huebner, "Roger Taney and the Slavery Issue," *Journal of American History* 97 (2010): 39–62.

45. Phillips, Fourth of July speech, Framingham, MA, July 4, 1859, in Stewart, *Phillips*, 191; on the schism with the Garrisonians, 196–97; on double vision, 198; on Phillips and Spooner: 200. On Douglass and Brown, Edward Ayers, *In the Presence of Mine Enemies: The Civil War in the Heart of America, 1859–1863* (New York: Norton, 2003), 15–16; on rebellion.

46. Spooner, "A Plan for the Abolition of Slavery (and) To the Non-Slaveholders of the South," 1858 (self-published pamphlet); Phillips, "Crispus Attucks and the Negroes," speech at Faneuil Hall, March 5, 1858, in Filler, ed., *Phillips*, 75; Jeffrey Rossbach, *Ambivalent Conspirators: John Brown, the Secret Six, and a Theory of Slave Violence* (Philadelphia: University of Pennsylvania Press, 1982), 3 and after; on lawlessness: David Grimsted, *American Mobbing, 1828–1861: Toward Civil War* (New York: Oxford University Press, 1998). Indian removals: Claudio Saunt, *Unworthy Republic* (New York: Norton, 2021); Richard Slotkin, *Regeneration through Violence: The Mythology of the American Frontier, 1600 1860* (Norman: University of Oklahoma Press, 1973), 517–63.

47. Phillips, "Eulogy of Brown," *National Anti-Slavery Standard*, November 19, 1859, p. 2. Brown's raid took place on federal land (the armory) and so fell under the Federal Crimes Act of 1790. He should have been tried by a federal court. Nevertheless, Col. Robert E. Lee of Virginia, whose federal troops arrested Brown and his fellow conspirators, took them to a Virginia jail, although the federal court for the Western District of Virginia was a mere 25 miles away. Virginia simply ignored that fact (as did the nearest federal judge, John Brockenbrough). See Peter Charles Hoffer, Williamjames Hoffer, and N. E. H. Hull, *The Federal Courts: An Essential History* (New York: Oxford University Press, 2016), 140–41. Phillips understood all of that, however.

48. "News of the Day," *New York Times*, November 2, 1859, p. 4. On Phillips's eulogy of Brown, Tony Horwitz, *Midnight Rising: John Brown and the Raid That Sparked the Civil War* (New York: Henry Holt, 2011), 261.

4. PATRIOT

1. Cicero, "Pro Milone," in *Cicero's Orations*, trans. Charles Duke Yonge (Raleigh, NC: Hayes Barton, 2005), 25; Phillip S. Paludan, "The American Civil War Considered as a Crisis in Law and Order," *American Historical Review* 77 (1972): 1013–34; Stephen C. Neff, *Justice in Blue and Gray: A Legal History of the Civil War* (Cambridge, MA: Harvard University Press, 2010), 4; Peter Charles Hoffer, *A Nation of Laws: America's Imperfect Pursuit of Justice* (Lawrence: University Press of Kansas, 2008), xi–xiii; but see William H. Rehnquist, *All the Laws But One: Civil Liberties in Wartime* (New York: Knopf, 1998), 221. (In time of war, some civil liberties are curbed.)

2. Hoffer, *Uncivil Warriors: The Lawyers' Civil War* (New York: Oxford University Press, 2018), 1–7.

3. Phillips, "The Pulpit," eulogy for Theodore Parker, November 18, 1860, in Pease, ed., *Speeches*, 2nd ser., 252, 266, 272, 274.

4. On South Carolina's secession, see Stephen A. Channing, *Crisis of Fear: Secession in South Carolina* (New York: Simon & Schuster, 1970), 261– 95; Michael P. Johnson, *Toward a Patriarchal Republic: The Secession of Georgia* (Baton Rouge: Louisiana State University Press, 1977), 17; and Christopher J. Olson, *Political Culture and Secession in Mississippi: Masculinity, Honor, and the Antiparty Tradition, 1830–1860* (New York: Oxford University Press, 2002), 187–94.

5. Phillips, "Argument for Disunion," January 20, 1861, in *Wendell Phillips on Civil Rights and Freedom*, ed. Louis Filler (New York: Hill and Wang, 1965), 115. Filler finds that Phillips's arguments were "moderately phrased, and more readily adapted to public debate" than Garrison's and Theodore Parker's version of disunionism. In fact, they were more legalistic rather than more moderate. On Seward's January speeches, see Seward, "The State of the Union," January 12, 1861, in *The Works of William Henry Seward*, ed. George E. Baker (New York, 1884), 4:662; and Seward, "The State of the Union," speech in the Senate, January 30, 1861, in George E. Baker, ed., *The Works of William H. Seward* (Boston: Houghton, Mifflin, 1884), 4:670, 672.

6. Phillips, "Argument for Disunion," 116; Phillips, "Progress," February 17, 1861, in *Speeches and Letters*, 2nd ser., 376, 381, 392; Bartlett, *Phillips*, 225–35, 236.

7. Phillips, "Dissolution of the Union," *New York Times*, March 21, 1861, p. 8.

8. Phillips, "Fourth of July Speech at Framingham," *New York Times*, July 13, 1861, p. 2.

9. Phillips, "Under the Flag," (the Music Hall speech) April 21, 1861, in Pease, ed., *Speeches*, 2nd ser., 396; Bartlett, *Phillips*, 236–37.

10. Phillips, "Under the Flag," 398.

11. Phillips, July Fourth Speech, 1861.

12. Phillips, July Fourth Speech, 1861.

13. Phillips, July Fourth Speech, 1861.

14. Phillips, July Fourth Speech, 1861; Stewart, *Phillips*, 219.

15. Phillips, July Fourth Speech, 1861.

16. Phillips, July Fourth Speech, 1861.

17. Phillips, July Fourth Speech, 1861; Benjamin Robbins Curtis, *Executive Power* (Boston: Little Brown, 1862).

18. Phillips, July Fourth Speech, 1861.

19. Phillips, "The Cabinet," August 1, 1862, in Pease, ed., *Speeches*, 2nd ser., 448; Bartlett, *Phillips*, 249–51, 253.

20. Phillips, "Emancipation," *Liberator*, January 9, 1863; *New York Herald*, January 1, 1863; Foner, *Fiery Trial*, 244–45; Phillips, "Letter," *New York Times*, August 8, 1863, p. 2, reporting a letter published in the *Liberator*, July 31, 1863.

21. Phillips, "Letter," *New York Times*, August 8, 1863. Well, perhaps it made sense to those conservative Republicans and apologists for slavery who opined that slavery was dying of its own accord.

22. Phillips, "Letter," 1863; Noah Feldman, *The Broken Constitution: Lincoln, Slavery, and the Refounding of America* (New York: Macmillan, 2022), argues that there were no grounds for preventing the seceding states from leaving, for there were no clear grounds for the Union's indissolubility.

23. Phillips, "Letter," 1863. The question of whether Phillips, despite his posture, was a racialist—that is, that he looked down on Black abolitionists and Black people in general—certainly is a valid one, and some Black leaders such as Frederick Douglass came to believe he was. At least one can find instances of condescension, or at least hypocrisy, in Phillips's pronouncements. The division over political action went even deeper. See, for example, Stephen Kantrowitz, *More Than Freedom: Fighting for Black Citizenship in a White Republic, 1829–1889* (New York: Penguin, 2012), 284; W. Caleb McDaniel, *The Problem of Democracy in the Age of Slavery: Garrisonian Abolitionists and Transatlantic Reform* (Baton Rouge: Louisiana State University Press, 2013), 160.

24. Phillips, "Letter," 1863. On the abolitionists and violence, see Lawrence J. Friedman, *Gregarious Saints: Self and Community in American Abolitionism* (New York: Cambridge University Press, 1982), 196–224.

25. Michael Les Benedict, "Wendell Phillips, the Constitution, and Constitutional Politics before the Civil War" in Aiséirithe and Yacovone, *Phillips*, 133–54.

26. Phillips, *Liberator*, January 1, 1864; Phillips, "The Immediate Issue," speech at the Boston Meeting of the Massachusetts Anti-Slavery Society, January 8, 1864, *New York Times*, January 9, 1864, p. 4. Phillips's early call for reparations is discussed fully and sympathetically in John David Smith's compendious forthcoming study of reparations.

27. Phillips, "Speech at the Women's Loyal National League," reported in the *New York Times*, February 16, 1864, p. 2; Phillips, *Liberator*, February 26, 1864, p. 1.

28. Phillips, "Women's Loyal League," p. 2.

29. Phillips, "Women's Loyal League."

30. Phillips, "Women's Loyal League."

31. Phillips, "The War, Its Cause and Its Cure," speech at Cooper Institute, *New York Times*, December 20, 1861, p. 8.

32. Phillips, "A Metropolitan Police," speech in Boston, April 5, 1863," in *Speeches and Letters*, 495, 497, 501, 502.

33. Phillips, in *National Anti-Slavery Standard*, May 14, 21, June 18, 1864.

34. Phillips, "The War, Its Cause and Cure"; Hoffer, *Seward's Law: Country Law, Relational Rights, and Slavery* (Ithaca, NY: Cornell University Press, 2023), 123–41.

35. Phillips, "The Immediate Issue," speech to the Boston Anti-Slavery Society, November 8, 1864, African American Pamphlet Collection, Library of Congress, Washington, DC.

36. Michael Vorenberg, *Final Freedom: The Civil War, the Abolition of Slavery, and the Thirteenth Amendment* (New York: Cambridge University Press, 2001), 130, 131, 134, 135, 180–87; Paul D. Escott, *Lincoln's Dilemma: Blair, Sumner, and the Republican Struggle over Racism and Equality in the Civil War Era* (Charlottesville: University of Virginia Press, 2014), 182–83; David E. Long, *The Jewel of Liberty: Abraham Lincoln's Re-election and the End of Slavery* (Mechanicsburg, PA: Stackpole, 1994), 153–77.

37. Bartlett, *Phillips*, 276–91.

5. ELDER STATESMAN

1. Eric Foner, *Reconstruction: America's Unfinished Revolution, 1863–1877* (New York: Harper, 1988), xxv; 258–59.

2. Michael Les Benedict, "Preserving the Constitution: The Conservative Basis of Radical Reconstruction," *Journal of American History* 61 (1974): 65–90; Harold M. Hyman and William M. Wieck, *Equal Justice Under Law, American Constitutional Development, 1835–1875* (New York: Harper, 1982), 298–99, 302–3, 322–23.

3. Seward, speech at Cooper Institution, February 22, 1866, in Baker, *Works* 5: 530, 531, 532, 533, 538. See also Hoffer, *Seward's Law*, 139–40, for text and references. Seward was one of the three members of Johnson's cabinet who remained after Johnson vetoed Republican Reconstruction legislation. Michael Les Benedict, *The Impeachment and Trial of Andrew Johnson* (New York: Norton, 1973), 15. In the cabinet, Seward had argued for a military trial for Jefferson Davis. Davis's legal counsel believed that Seward hated Davis with a passion. Cynthia Nicoletti, *Secession on Trial: The Treason Prosecution of Jefferson Davis* (New York: Cambridge University Press, 2017), 71–72.

4. Howell Cobb to his wife, December 7, 1865, in *Correspondence of Robert Toombs, Alexander H. Stephens and Howell Cobb*, ed. Ulrich Bonnell Phillips (Washington, DC: US Government Printing Office, 1913), 672; Alexander Stephens to J. Barrett Cohen, July 4, 1866, 681; docket books for the Northern District of Georgia, 1865–1866, NARA Atlanta (Morrow), Georgia; Foner, *Reconstruction*, 209; W. Lewis Burke Jr., "The Radical Law School: The University of

South Carolina School of Law and Its African American Graduates, 1873–1877," in *At Freedom's Door: African American Founding Fathers and Lawyers in Reconstruction South Carolina*, ed. Lewis W. Burke and James L. Underwood (Columbia: University of South Carolina Press, 2000), 90–115. See also Hoffer, *Uncivil Warriors*, 170–72, for text and citations.

5. Henry Raymond, editorial, *New York Times*, June 10, 1865, p. 4.

6. Stewart, *Phillips*, 277–80. That legacy begot Jim Crow legislation throughout the South. Public spaces, public facilities, and state and local politics were segregated, denying equality to those freed by the Thirteenth Amendment and undermining the protections of the Fourteenth and Fifteenth Amendments. Jim Crow would have been impossible without law—statutes, ordinances, and the enforcement mechanisms of legal offices. In a terrible irony, Jim Crow turned Phillips's positivism and strong democracy on their heads.

7. Wendell Phillips, *National Anti-Slavery Standard*, December 8, 1866, p. 1; on one occasion the bodyguards were supplied by Harvard College friends of Oliver Wendell Holmes Jr. Douglas R. Egerton, *Thunder at the Gates: The Black Civil War Regiments That Redeemed America* (New York: Basic, 2016), 1, 4, 31. On another occasion, members of a radical German union provided bodyguards. Mark Peterson, *The City-State of Boston: The Rise and Fall of an Atlantic Power, 1630–1865* (Princeton, NJ: Princeton University Press, 2019), 621. The metaphor of the melting pot was introduced in Israel Zangwell's 1908 play *The Melting Pot*. It implied that all human differences could be melted into one universally acceptable type of citizen. Zangwell was an English author and the play, about America, opened in London and traveled to New York City the next year.

8. Phillips, [Untitled], *National Anti-Slavery Standard*, January 4, 1868, p. 2; Phillips, "The Elections," *New York Times*, November 12, 1868, p. 1; Phillips, "The Elections," *National Anti-Slavery Standard*, November 13, 1869, p. 2; Stewart, *Phillips*, 272–77.

9. U. S. Grant, Special Message to Congress, March 23, 1871, American Presidency Project, https://www.presidency.ucsb.edu/documents/special-message-2176, accessed 8/3/23; Foner, *Reconstruction*, 444–59.

10. Phillips, "The Negro's Claim," *National Anti-Slavery Standard*, January 29, 1870; see Roy E. Finkenbine, "Wendell Phillips and 'The Negro's Claim': A Neglected Reparations Document," *Massachusetts Historical Review* 7 (2005): 105–19; and Risa Goluboff, *The Lost Promise of Civil Rights* (Cambridge: Harvard University Press, 2007), 9.

11. Timothy Messer-Kruse, "Eight Hours, Greenbacks, and 'Chinamen': Wendell Phillips, Ira Steward, and the Fate of Labor Reform in Massachusetts," *Labor History* 42, no. 2 (2001): 134; Phillips, "The Foundation of the Labor Movement," speech in Worcester, Massachusetts September 4, 1871, in Pease, ed., *Speeches,*

2nd ser., 154; Phillips, "The Labor Question," April 1872, Pease, ed., *Speeches*, 2nd ser., 171; Samuel Bernstein, "Wendell Phillips, Labor Advocate," *Science and Society* 20 (1956): 344–57.

12. Phillips, speech at the Ninth National American Women's Suffrage Association, New York, May 12, 1859, Proceedings of the National American Women's Suffrage Association.

13. Phillips, "Women's Rights and Women's Duties," speech in New York, May 10, 1866, in *Speeches on the Rights of Women* (Philadelphia: Alfred Ferris, 1899), 56, 62, 63; Stewart, *Phillips*, 265.

14. Stewart, *Phillips*, 282–89; Faye E. Dudden, *Fighting Chance: The Struggle over Women Suffrage and Black Suffrage in Reconstruction America* (New York: Oxford University Press, 2011), 62; N. E. H. Hull, *The Woman Who Dared to Vote: The Trial of Susan B. Anthony* (Lawrence: University Press of Kansas, 2012), 4–18.

15. Phillips, "Speech of May 19, 1866," *National Anti-Slavery Standard*, p. 2.

16. Phillips, "The Chinese," editorial, *National Anti-Slavery Standard*, July 30, 1870, p. 2.

17. Phillips, "The Chinese."

18. Madeline Bilis, "Throwback Thursday: Maine Become the First State to Outlaw Liquor" Boston City Life, https://www.bostonmagazine.com/news/2016/06/02/maine-alcohol-history/, accessed 8/7/23; Phillips, "The Maine Liquor Law," February 28, 1865, in *Speeches*, 2nd ser., 181, 186, 190. Mark Wahlgren Summers, *The Plundering Generation: Corruption and the Crisis of the Union, 1849–1861* (New York: Oxford University Press, 1988), 199.

19. Phillips, "William Lloyd Garrison," in Pease, ed., *Speeches*, 2nd ser., 459, 461, 464, 468.

6. THE DUTY OF A SCHOLAR IN A REPUBLIC

1. Phillips, "An Address before the Association of the Ministers of the Methodist Episcopal Church, in Tremont Temple, Boston, January 24, 1881," Pease, *Speeches*, 2nd ser., 195.

2. Phillips, "The Duty of a Scholar in a Republic," speech at Harvard Phi Beta Kappa Bicentennial, June 30, 1881, Pease, *Speeches*, 2nd ser., 331. "We must think things, not words," Oliver Wendell Holmes, Jr., "Law in Science and Science in Law," *Harvard Law Review* 12 (1899): 120.

3. On five-foot bookshelf: *The Five Foot Shelf of Books (The Harvard Classics), Collected by Charles W. Eliot*, 14 vol. (New York: Colliers, 1909).

4. Phillips, "Scholar," 331.

5. Phillips, "Scholar," 332.

6. Phillips, "Scholar," 332.

7. Phillips, "Scholar," 333; Herbert Butterfield, *The Whig Interpretation of History* (1931; repr., New York: Norton, 1965), 11: "It is part and parcel of the Whig interpretation of history that it studies the past with reference to the present." No better example can be found than Phillips's use of history. And his heroizing of Vane and others also fit the model. Butterfield, *Whig*, 34: "The result [of Whig history] is that to many of us [historical figures] seem much more modern than they really were."

8. Philips, "Scholar," 334. On slavery in New England, Wendy Warren, *New England Bound: Slavery and Colonization in Early America* (New York: Norton, 2016). Recapitulation theory posits that the development of an individual organism (ontogeny) follows (recapitulates) the same phases of the evolution of that organism's species (phylogeny). It was popularized in the late nineteenth century by Ernst Haeckel. G. Stanley Hall adopted it in his widely read *Adolescence* (1904).

9. Phillips, "Scholar," 334.

10. Phillips, "Scholar," 336.

11. Phillips, "Scholar," 337.

12. Phillips, "Scholar," 337.

13. Phillips, "Scholar," 338; "Wendell Phillips on Legal Abuses," *Albany Bar Journal* 5 (1872): 17, 33.

14. Phillips, "Scholar," 338–39; Larry Gara, "Horace Mann: Anti-Slavery Congressman," *Historian* 32 (1969): 25–26, 27, 31; Horace Mann, "Means and Objects of a Common School Education," in *Life and Works of Horace Mann* (Boston: Lee and Shepard, 1891), 2: 83–84; Samuel May Jr. to Samuel Joseph May, March 5, 1853, Boston Public Library; A. D. Mayo, "Horace Mann and the Great Revival of the Common School in American," *Report of the Commissioner of Education, for the Year 1896–1897* (Washington, DC: Bureau of Education, 1898), 1: 731; Benedict, "Phillips," in Aiséirithe and Yacovone, *Phillips*, 142. The dispute featured Phillips, defending the supremacy of the Supreme Court, and Mann, who sat in Congress, arguing that the Supreme Court was not the final arbiter.

15. Phillips, "Scholar," 342.

16. Phillips, "Scholar," 344.

17. Phillips, "Scholar," 345.

18. Phillips, "Scholar," 347.

19. Phillips, "Scholar," 347.

20. Phillips, "Scholar," 348.

21. Phillips, "Scholar," 349.

22. Phillips, "Scholar," 351, 357.

CONCLUSION

1. See, for example, Moritz Pinner to Wendell Phillips, June 1, 1860, Wendell Phillips Papers, 1855–1882 (MS Am 1953), Houghton Library, Harvard University. On the power of self-respect as a motivator, see Nathaniel Brandon, *The Six Pillars of Self-Esteem* (New York: Bantam, 1995).

2. By the antebellum era, New England's was a guilt culture as opposed to a shame culture. See John Demos, "Shame and Guilt in Early New England" in *The Emotions: Social, Cultural, and Biological Dimensions*, ed. Rom Harré and W. Gerard Parrott (London: Sage, 1996), 74–88. In contrast, the South's elite was becoming more and more shame conscious: Bertram Wyatt-Brown, *Southern Honor: Ethics and Behavior in the Old South*, 25th anniv. ed. (New York: Oxford University Press, 2007), 5 and after.

3. Phillips, Remarks of Wendell Phillips at the Funeral of William Lloyd Garrison, March 28, 1879 (Boston: Lee and Shepard, 1884), 3, 4, 5, 6, 11; Philips, "Eulogy of Charles Sumner," *New York Times*, March 19, 1877, p. 2.

4. This is no place for an essay on social injustice in the twenty-first century, or for an essay that rings with Phillips-like moral indignation. Outrage history and imagined history are fantasies that revel in our own "philippics." But who can doubt that Phillips speaks to our own day? On controversies over presentism today, see, for example, David Armitage, "In Defense of Presentism" in *History and Human Flourishing*, ed. Darrin M. McMahon (Oxford: Oxford University Press 2022), 59–84; James H. Sweet, "Is History History? Identity Politics and Teleologies of the Present," *Perspectives on History*, August 17, 2022; David I. Bell, "Two Cheers for Presentism," *Chronicle of Higher Education*, August 23, 2022.

5. Gregory Ablavsky and W. Tanner Allread, "We the (Native) People: How Indigenous Peoples Debated the U. S. Constitution," *Columbia Law Review* 123 (2023): 44, 45; Ariela Gross, "When Is the Time of Slavery? The History of Slavery in Contemporary Legal and Political Argument," *California Law Review* 96 (2008): 41; Louis Michael Seidman, "American's Racial Stain: The Taint Argument and the Limits of Constitutional Law and Rhetoric," *American Journal of Law and Equality* 2 (2022): 165; W. Kerrel Murray, "Discriminatory Taint," *Harvard Law Review* 135 (2022): 81.

6. Phillips, "The Lost Arts," 1881, in Pease, ed., *Speeches*, 2nd ser., 366, 369, 394, 397.

7. Phillips, "Lost Arts," 398.

Index